THE NEW YORK CITY SUBWAYS' MOTORMANS' RANT

TORIN REID

authorHOUSE®

AuthorHouse™
1663 Liberty Drive
Bloomington, IN 47403
www.authorhouse.com
Phone: 1 (800) 839-8640

Published by AuthorHouse 11/29/2019

ISBN: 978-1-7283-3815-6 (sc)
ISBN: 978-1-7283-3813-2 (hc)
ISBN: 978-1-7283-3814-9 (e)

Library of Congress Control Number: 2019919340

Print information available on the last page.

This book is printed on acid-free paper.

CONTENTS

INTRODUCTION

Day after working day, the view from the New York City Subway motorman's cab is roughly the same. Looking out through the weathered front window, the motorman sees, in between stretches of dark tunnel or open air elevated, the faces of thousands of New York City subway riders at the stations. The faces of the riders reflect many different moods upon their seeing the oncoming subway train. The expression that I saw the most was that of contempt.

The look upon my face when I was driving the train (I am now retired) is that of indifference. I have realized a long time ago, that 95% of the time, the attitude of the riders is misplaced. Along with the bus driver, the vanishing station agent, the subway conductor (who opens and closes the trains doors) and the subway motorman (now more widely known as the train operator - the person who drives the train) all get the blame for whatever goes wrong within the Transit system. It does not matter whether blaming any or all these workers makes any sense.

Perhaps it is a little repetitive to say this here, but it needs to be said. The bus driver did not create the traffic jam. The train operator and conductor did not create the sick passenger. Nor did they, along with the station agent, create the infamous service diversions (disruptions?) that occur every night and weekend. And, the station agent did not create the rise in fares.

But, all of the above is not the reason why I have written this book. The far larger purpose of this book is for you, the New York City subway or bus rider (and everybody else) to get a better understanding of what is really going on every time you descend into the darkness or ascend those steep elevated stairs.

But to get that better understanding of what is really going on within the subways, I need you – the reader – to get beyond the usual knee jerk reactions and outright ignorance that populate most of the current thinking about the subways.

I can tell you, right now, what is wrong with the state of New York City subways. Basically, there are two main reasons why the New York subways are the way that they are. The first reason is that the first customer of the MTA – not just the NYC subways – is NOT the passenger – it is the contractor or sub-contractor. And this is nothing new. It has been this way for the past 15 or 20 years. All the various contractors or sub-contractors have been sucking the MTA – and, therefore, New York state and the taxpayers dry for many years.

In this instance, we can think of the subways as a man in the jungle who has fallen into a swamp pond. He is able to make it out of the swamp, but now, he is covered with blood sucking leeches. He now staggers over to a tent, otherwise known as 2 Broadway, the MTA Headquarters building. Within this tent he sinks into a chair. An MTA doctor takes away some of the leeches. The man, now weakened, cannot seem to leave his chair. The "doctor" is busy applying new, stronger and greedier leeches to his helpless patient, while telling him that, in time, the leeches will make you feel better.

The suits and ties people within the upper echelons of 2 Broadway hand out contracts like so many sweet lollipops to contractors who have not previously set foot in a subway. I wonder, are they getting kickbacks for this behavior? Yet both groups, the vice presidents and the contractors, enjoy long belly laughs over champagne as the tabloid news media trumpet over a few well- placed union employees who made thousands in overtime.

And the second reason why the New York subway is the way it is, is because the subway is made up on different departments, none of whom work together. I strongly suspect but I cannot prove, that this particular form of internal dysfunction dates back to the early 1990's during the time when Peter Kalikow, a real estate developer was at the head of the MTA. I believe that Mr. Kalikow, fearful of the power of numbers and faced with the threat of a strike from what was then a relatively strong and united Transport Workers Union, successfully sought to break up the unity of those times by having department heads introduce policies and directives that often set one department at odds with another. Since those times, we now have at least two generations of workers that work, but not necessarily with each other. If two departments work together on a project, it is because they have been forced to work together or that someone saw some kind of mutual benefit of working together.

As another analogy, let us now think of a symphony orchestra (or may be just a musical band) that is attempting to make music without a musical conductor or even a band leader. Now each section of the orchestra is committed to making their own personal "music", sometimes as loud as possible. But each departments "music", is set to their own personal drumbeat. The result is that you and I and the rest of the public hears a lot of noise. And, dear subway rider, if you are only half aware, you can "see" a lot of the noise for yourself, every time that you are redirected to a shuttle bus because of a service diversion. For those readers who are not in New York, don't worry, please read on and I will back up what I wrote, other than my suspicions about the era of Mr. Kalikow.

In the past 15 or 20 years, there have been dozens and perhaps hundreds of construction projects that have veered from the necessary to the dubious on through to the ridiculous. Someone needs to erect a McDonalds type of sign that flashes "billions and billions spent", in front of the building at 2 Broadway.

Most New Yorkers – including those with power – hear all of this "noise". But, like a car alarm in the middle of the night, they simply wish it would go away. And there are those that have the knowledge – many with more knowledge than me - to silence this "alarm" and make everything run right. But these people are usually working for the MTA and they don't want to interrupt their personal cash flow. And so, the noise continues, and the contractors and the MTA top management insist that the riders and the taxpayers pony up yet more money for another subway "fix".

One might say, well, aren't you retired? Why do you even care? Why don't you just pack up and go down south or to Florida/Arizona/North Carolina, etc., like everyone else? Well, there's just that small matter of me liking the subway trains. Ever since I was a kid. And then there is the adult realization that under that dirt and piss and rats lies one of the five best railroads on Earth. No one seems to recognize that.

Now, all you have to do is take your metro card and swipe it, listen for the beep that indicates that you just bought this book, and head on down the stairs (or up to the platform) for a far more enlightened ride then you are used to.

Oh! And there is one more point that I have to make. This book will discuss subway trains and railroads at length. I will try and present this material as if I am addressing the lay person, or someone who knows only a little about this subject. Please keep this in mind. And, you might need a New York City subway map if you are not familiar with the subway system.

Torin Reid

June 10, 2019

IN THE BEGINNING

I have to admit, that I may have stuffed a lot of material into the preceding introduction. In this beginning, I am going to set up the next few chapters by discussing people – yes, people. By discussing the people first, I can give you a broader and better insight into why the subway system is the way it is. The people that are relevant to the New York City subway fall into three categories. The three groups are: the riders, the workers, and the management. Each group depends upon the other two groups to make the subways function. This is true in New York as it is in most other transportation companies in the world. But in New York, the three groups, the riders, the workers and the management do not trust one another. At times, each of the three groups can be openly contemptuous of the other two. When you think about it and look at the current newspaper articles, most of you readers will agree with me.

It is important that we discuss people first in this book, so that we can get a closer look at the problems. The heart of any transportation enterprise, or indeed, any select group of human beings such as a baseball team or even the man and wife who decide to host at barbeque for family and friends, will always be the people, especially those "in charge".

Everything else – all the hardware – in these examples, all of the trains, tracks, buses and stations for the subway, all of the balls, bats and stadiums for the baseball team, and all of the burgers, hot dogs, sodas and beers from the barbeque hosts. All of these are just tools with which they need to get the tasks at hand accomplished.

Now, the hardware will have its place within the book, but that will come later. It is much more important to discuss people, and the effects that they leave behind, right now. Let us start with the management, who for the purposes of this book is leaving all of us with the subway's capital plans. This is why I detail a few of those projects right away. Then, I discuss the employees, especially those from other departments, and finally, the passengers (yes, you the subway passenger).

THE MANAGEMENT

The Management

Within the next series of essays, I would like to think like to think that I might reach those within the upper echelons of subways management (such as the department heads and above) and inform them (it seems to me like some are clueless) of the effects of their management or non-management. And, while it would be exciting and somewhat titillating to write about some of the more colorful characters that I have come across within management, I believe that it would be more effective to write about how things are seen from the end consumer, that is, the passenger and sometimes, the employees' view of things. Besides that, when I was working in the subway, I was in what they called RTO (Rapid Transit Operations, now known as Service Delivery). Most of my interactions with higher level management were infrequent and limited at best. But I had plenty of time during the workday to observe the work of the other managers of other departments (such as Track and Infrastructure) and their effects upon the passengers of my trains.

While I am at it, I will have to go against some of the stereotypes as seen by my blue-collar co-workers. Not every superintendent or manager was an asshole or a power freak, although I once witnessed a superintendent interfere with the switching of subway cars at East New York Yard. Many of the supervisors that I met were responsible people trying to do their jobs. Indeed, I remember three superintendents that were, to me, outstanding individuals. I will name them here as Mr. W., Mr. S., and Mrs. P. All were from RTO/Service Delivery. I believed that all three should have continued upwards into top management. I believe all would have made a difference. They were all upright and principled people. Perhaps that was the reason why they were not selected for further promotion.

On the other hand, they are some things that are right in front of all of our faces that are clear management and upper management failures. When you see a rotting stairway, a crumbling platform, or cancerous looking station wall tiles, this is because of an upper management indecision or non-decision. When you see a totally neglected station such as Chambers Street or the J and M lines crumbling like some kind of Roman ruin while other, less damaged stations get refurbished, this is a management failure at 2 Broadway (MTA NYC Transit HQ) far away from RTO/Service Delivery. When the construction contractors get to pick and choose exactly which stations rehab jobs that they want, this is a failure of top management to supervise. With the stations, I could go on and on. Think of Court Square on the G line in Queens. The tunnel walls were rotting with brown leaks and so on at the station platforms last time I looked. Only the upper level of that station had been refurbished. The 205th Street/Norwood Station in the Bronx is an insult to the neighborhood above it. And this, my friends, is after at least four, five-year Capital Plans in which billions and billions of dollars were spent. And, this type of construction dysfunction exists not just with the stations, but nearly everywhere else within the subways.

Rather than say, "Superintendent Jones" is responsible for this, or "Vice President Allen" is responsible for that, I prefer to point out the effects of bad management or non-management so that it is easier for anyone to see what has gone wrong.

My fantasy is that, someone in power would read at least this section of the book and then become more introspective and make better decisions within the subways. Let's start with how people – the passengers – the lifeblood of the subways —are treated, with those infamous service diversions.

"I have to Fuck with the Trains"

Dear reader, if you are a New York City subway rider, I'm pretty sure that you will understand the above quote, from a fellow subway patron. If you happen to be a transit employee who works within the department (Operations Planning, actually) that covers service diversions and general orders, feel free to cut out this entire essay, and attach it to your rulebook or place the pages behind glass in your employee break room. If you, the reader, are not from either of these two groups, don't worry, because I will explain why such a pedestrian quote has to be explained at all. The goal of this entire essay is to convey the frustrations that the average subway rider has whenever he or she encounters a service diversion. Allow me to direct your focus, for the sake of clarity, on just one line, the N line. After you have read the next few essays, you can then multiply the frustration by all of the subway lines. So now (for the second time) here is that quote:

"I have to fuck with the trains!" bellowed this man on his cell phone while riding a northbound N train towards 8th Avenue Station, on a sunny day. I remember this conversation very clearly because he was sitting across from me in the subway car. Of course, I was in my full transit uniform. And it was clear that this man wanted me to know about his problems. Perhaps it was his wife or girlfriend who was on the other end of this conversation. The man continued on the phone with "I'm sorry baby, but on Saturday, I don't know when I will get there. Then he repeated, "I have to fuck with the trains! I don't know which way they are going".

This poster shows the service diversions that occur within the New York City subways on a regular basis. These are the service diversions for just one week in August, 2019. Photo – Torin Reid

Again, to those of you who ride the subways - you know, more or less what that man was talking about. For the rest of us in the world, and that includes the MTA Operations Planning management, (I need those MTA guys to read this essay twice) let me explain.

The phrase "I have to fuck with the trains!" means, more or less, in New Yorkese, that this man contemplates having to endure the wasted time and energy of having to be forced to travel in the opposite direction, or rerouted from one subway line to another or to a shuttle bus, going far from where he was used to, in order to get where he wanted to go. Alternatively, another translation could be when one has to contemplate the possibility that regular train service has been interrupted.

Well, some people might say, that angry man could have been a nutty model train hobbyist, ranting about his model train layout. The answer to that is no. Most model train guys don't shout their hobby out, not in public. Rather than that, this man was thinking about the effects of the ongoing MTA service diversions on the N line. In this particular service diversion, trains on the N line ran express in one direction, skipping several stations, while trains running in the opposite direction made all the local stops. While this particular service diversion had been going on for a couple of weeks, it still meant that many unsuspecting subway riders were forced to ride a train in the opposite direction from where they were headed to, just to get that train that they needed to get where they were going. And, the passengers who had not found out about the service diversions beforehand meant that they did not plan for all the wasted time, and therefore, they were going to get to their destinations late.

Like it or not, it is simply a fact of the mass transit life that many people expect to simply show up at a subway (or bus, or whatever) station at any time and expect that the subway or bus will take them where they are going. For those of you within the MTA Operations Planning department, please be advised, that this is not an unreasonable expectation. Indeed, from a passenger service point of view, continuous, 24 hour service should be just that, continuous, 24 hour service. Service diversions should be kept to an absolute minimum, not a maximum, not whenever you or the contractors feel like it. It does not matter how many alternative routes are posted (if they are posted at all). There will always be a significant group of people who will show up at a particular station, expecting to get where they had planned to go. Most of the people are casual, not daily riders. Some simply didn't pay attention to the service diversion signs wherever they were posted.

Some people can't be bothered or don't know how to look online for MTA service updates. In any case, any extended service diversion will create a significant group of people who will now hate the subways or dismiss the service as unreliable. These people will plan their future commutes by automobile, contributing to the weekday gridlock that is endemic within New York City. For many New Yorkers, sitting for 30 minutes in an Uber or Lyft vehicle going 10 miles per hour is a preferable to riding miles out of one's way on the subway or a shuttle bus.

Now, let's get back to that man with the big mouth on the N train. When we look a little deeper at his phone conversation – "I'm sorry baby, but on Saturday I don't know how I'll get there" – it looks like this man felt that he had no alternative, or did not think of any of the bus lines as an alternative to getting to see his significant other on Saturday. He may have not had the money to pay for a Uber or Lyft vehicle.

Alternatively, this man, with some research and a brisk walk, could have used the somewhat nearby D train (West End) line, to get close to where he wanted to go. But most New Yorkers see the subway or bus system only through that one or maybe two services that they always use. Thus, that man, with his self-imposed limited choices, saw no other way out. This made him angry. The only way that he could express himself, in a New York way is to say, "I have to fuck with the trains".

Piss them off, 150 at a time! Every 10 minutes!

Now, in the previous essay on the 'N' line, I was all set to title it "The effects of the Service Diversions – Part 1". But I could not resist giving that essay the title that it has now. And that also explains why this essay has the title that it does instead of ("…Part II"). So, now here we go.

Let us extend that stay on the 'N' line for just a little bit longer. Let us look at another facet of the passenger's reactions to the effects of the same set of service diversions. (Most transit people call these service diversions "G.O.'s for General Orders, but I am writing for the layman).

So, let us again visit that northbound 'N' train that has been skipping those stations on the open-air portion of the line in Brooklyn. However, this fresh, new incident happened on a different day. This time, I was operating the train.

After skipping all those stations, my 'N' train was now on an embankment, just past 8th Avenue. The train descends slowly into the tunnel that lies under a portion of the Brooklyn-Queens Expressway. At this point, astute observers can still spot the remnants of one of Brooklyn's old elevated lines, which diverged from the Sea Beach line (Today's 'N' line).

Within the tunnel, the train follows a sharp right-hand turn curve. The trains' direction changes from westbound to northbound as the train arrives on the express track. Lo and behold, a northbound 'R' train is also arriving at the 59th street and 4th Avenue station on the local track. Both trains stop at the platform at nearly the same time. An across the platform connection is possible. Without any prompting about 150 people scamper out the local train to the open doors of the express train. Logically, they all feel the express train will get them into the city a little faster.

But, wait! The yellow holding lights come on for the 'N' train signaling to the conductor on the express train that he should keep the doors open. These holding lights are at most major stations. The purpose of these holding lights is to allow the subway control tower that governs this track (in this case, Murphy Tower, located near the Ninth Ave station on the present D line) to control and halt train traffic if need be.

So, there we sit. The local train closes its doors and rushes out of the station. It does not take a physic to feel the collective surprise, and the anger from the passengers, wafting out from the body of the subway cars.

I was not aware of this at that time but all of the northbound 'N' trains were being held there at 59ᵗʰ street and 4ᵗʰ Avenue until such time as the train matched its regularly scheduled departure time from there (as if the train made all of the above ground stops on the 'N' line instead of skipping those stations) from the 59ᵗʰ street and 4ᵗʰ avenue station.

Now, it is one thing if I didn't know what was going on. I just had to sit there with the train, and I was getting paid anyway. But it is quite another thing for the passengers of the train to sit and wait. Does anybody remember the old Seinfeld comedy show episode about the subways? Especially the part where Elaine (actress Julia Louis-Dreyfus) runs through all of her angst during the few minutes in which the train car is not moving?

Anyway, those holding lights stayed on for seven long minutes, which is an eternity within the New York City subway. An announcement by the conductor (the person who opens and closes the doors) that "were being held here by the dispatcher" was now only gasoline upon the mental fires of each passenger who ran off the 'R' train.

By the time we left the station, many of the passengers were thoroughly upset. And I knew this, even though hardly anyone said a word.

But then it got worse. That same Murphy Tower that I mentioned earlier, now decides to hold my train just south of the 36th street and 4th avenue station, another stop where the express and the local trains meet, and the 'D' (West End) service joins the 4th avenue line. Now of course, the tower routed a northbound 'D' train into that station ahead of my train.

By now, it should be apparent to the lay person reading this essay that the train operator (the person who drives the train) and the conductor (the person who opens and closes the doors) are not the only ones in charge of the subway trains over the road from one terminal to another. Indeed, running a subway train in New York is akin to running from one electronic fiefdom (the control towers) to another which is controlled by an unseen, Wizard of Oz like character, who, in reality with their cloaks removed, are transit workers just like us. The tower operators and their supervisors are out of sight and far removed from "the road". Therefore, they do not see the human ramifications of their decisions. The responsibility for dealing with the public is left up to the conductors mostly, and the train operators.

So, that 'D' train leaves the 36th street and 4th avenue station, none too quickly, I might add. Once we enter into that station, we encounter holding lights once again. There is no real reason to do this, as the signal system will keep the trains separated. Upon seeing these holding lights, the conductor once again makes the perfunctory station announcement. "We are being held by supervision…" This time I can hear the tongue clucking and sighing from inside the trains' operating cab. And then there is one more reaction. "Move the fucking train!" Someone from within the train has lost it. "C'mon, goddammit, let's go!", this person bellows. And, lo and behold, the conductor makes another announcement and closes the train doors. So apparently to everyone inside the car, the expletive filled tirade seems to have worked. After all, it is the train operator and the conductor who are responsible for moving the train, right? Please note that I am being a little sarcastic here.

Now, the train arrives at Atlantic Avenue – Barclays Center. Once upon a time this station was called Pacific Street. In between the last express station (36th Street and 4th Avenue) and Atlantic Avenue, the train has crossed the unseen electronic boundary that separates one control tower from another. This new electronic fiefdom is now ruled by DeKalb Avenue tower, a totally hidden fortress deep within the bowels of that station. The DeKalb Avenue tower, apparently unaware of the decisions made by the preceding Murphy Tower, turns on the holding lights again at Atlantic Avenue. The only logical reason that I can think of them doing this, is that they want to route a 'Q' or 'B' train in front of me, as the Brighton line tracks join the complex before most of the trains cross the Manhattan Bridge. Of course, the passengers don't understand what is going on. To tell you the truth, I as the train operator didn't know what the hell was going on, that they have to hold my train back so much. And to make things even worse, there was that local train across the platform at Atlantic Avenue – Barclay Center. This was the same local 'R' train that left us behind at 59th Street and 4th Avenue. And now, that same 'R' train was leaving the station and leaving us behind once again. The screamer within my train became out of control. "Will you move the motherfucking train, please!? Why don't you stop fucking around!!??" Then this man started to slam his fists against the windows and walls to the to the train. No one stopped him or spoke out against him. Most of the people silently agreed with him. When he started banging on the operating cab door, that was enough for me. I opened the door and I gave back to this guy what he gave to me. "Do you see the motherfucking red signal?" and that's all I will say about that incident.

Needless to say, a fair amount of the assaults and verbal abuse that is directed at the conductor and train operator starts out this way, through someone's frustration at the pace of the train traffic. I hope that by relating this example to you, the reader can get a better idea of what actually goes on within the system. And tell your asshole friends to stop abusing the train crews. Subway delays are usually not their fault. If you wish to direct your anger at the MTA, email it or twitter it to 2 Broadway, (MTA Headquarters) where it might make a difference.

And, finally, do you know what? To solve this entire problem, and diffuse all of that collective anger, all that a supervisor – a train station dispatcher back at Coney Island – the beginning of the line - had to do was delay the 'N' train's departure time from the Coney Island terminal by seven minutes. This way, no one would have even known that there was a problem.

How much is enough?

This is yet another continuation from the previous essay. We're still on that 'N' line. After we have considered the view of that one passenger, and the other passengers, we must now consider the view of the MTA and its' contractors.

One might consider that the work on the 'N' line stations had to be done. Prior to the refurbishment program, 'N' line "Sea Beach" stations were in poor condition, with peeling paint and small hunks of concrete falling from the ceilings to the station platforms or roadbed. Clearly, the work needed to be done. But, at what price should this work be done? Did the MTA get at least some value for what it has paid? Has the costs of the service disruption been figured into the total amount? (I have a figure of $325 million dollars, for six stations to be refurbished on the N line). Have the human costs - the resultant anger and time wasted – been figured into this amount? I doubt it. Has anyone paid attention to the work going on nearby subway lines that might have been useful alternatives, so that people might have another way to get to work? (In my view, the answer is no).

I have to pose this question to those employees who work within the New York City Subways' Service

Diversions (to them, General Orders) department. How much is enough? Have you ever attempted to figure out how many service diversions are going on one subway line within a calendar year? Has anybody been keeping track? How many weekends and/or weekdays must one "fuck with the trains" before the riding public get tired and ridership falls permanently?

Has anybody with that flood prone edifice otherwise known as 2 Broadway ever thought of doing such a study?

Probably not. I suspect that the ridership loss of upset subway passengers begins with those people who can afford to switch to Uber or Lyft, at least on the weekends. And then there are those who already have their own cars, who finally make the decision to sit in the traffic and pay for the parking at one end of their commutes – and sometimes, both ends of their commutes. Generally speaking, the subway may not see these passengers again. And while I have concentrated on the N line, when you multiply these headaches and service diversions by all of the subway lines, you can begin to understand some of the public feelings about the subways.

In my opinion, when you see service diversions on a subway line more than, say, 8 to 10 weekends out of a 52 week year, I believe that a more or less permanent erosion of ridership will begin on that line. With all of the talk of "New Technology" being thrown around, I openly wonder why some of this New Technology has not been aimed at a more efficient way of subway reconstruction.

Has anybody driven upon the streets of this city lately? The city streets are choked all over, at a minimum, from 7am until at least 7pm. This goes for the highways as well as the main arteries within the city. The city streets might resemble those in Mumbai or Calcutta (actually Kolkata) as the traffic chokes the daily life and drives up the costs of doing business in New York City. And, not for nothing, but both Mumbai and Kolkata have both opened brand new subway systems. But back in the streets of New York, there are hundreds, probably even thousands of people who could not take even one more service diversion and have abandoned the subway, probably forever. This means that this person has given up their two square feet of standing room on a subway train, with their 120 to let's say, 300 average pounds of body weight. Now, they occupy a six foot by eighteen foot space – and 4000 or more pounds plus their body weight – and that of the cars' driver — on the crumbling city streets above in a car. Not only that, but the spaces that the cars occupy is being made ever more restrictive through the use of bike lanes. Someone thinks that if they add enough bike lanes that this city will turn into Amsterdam. Another crock are these school zone speed cameras. Have you ever noticed that those school zone speed cameras don't really protect the school zones? Instead, they are located hundreds of feet away from the schools. They are marketed to the public as traffic calming devises. They are actually, like the fire hydrant where the exclusion zone is not clearly marked, financial automobile pimping objects for the City of New York.

The Effects of People Not using the Subways

Let me relate to you a phenomenon that I have personally witnessed. What I saw backs up what I have just said about the subways, and how the negative perceptions of the subways by the public contributes to traffic congestion with the city.

As is known by nearly everyone on the planet, July 4th is a federal holiday. Within New York City, everyone there knows about the city's main July 4th fireworks display on the East River (In the past, it was on the Hudson) that is sponsored by Macy's department store.

Somewhat less known by most of the general public is that there are many more 4th of July celebrations within the surrounding suburbs. There are even a few within the outlying areas of the city itself. Most of the fireworks displays occur at around the same time and place as the main fireworks show in Manhattan. These smaller outlying fireworks displays are well attended because not everyone wants to make that extra trip to Manhattan and get penned in like cattle.

So, it was with the July 4th, 2018 celebration at Coney Island. There, the celebration was smaller and the people somewhat more relaxed, I think, then at the one in Manhattan because food and drink we readily available. And there is one other reason. I believe that Coney Island is readily accessible by automobile, and you don't have to "fuck with the trains" (Ok, I won't use that phrase any more) on that long trip to Manhattan.

The main problem with the Coney Island July 4th fireworks displays was how people got there. Everyone drove, and I mean everyone. While the half empty subway trains and buses arrived and departed at the large Stillwell Avenue bus terminal, cars begin to fill, and then clog the streets around Coney Island. First, all the regular spots disappeared between Surf and Neptune Avenue. Then, all the backstreet spots, in the darkened streets between Surf Avenue and Neptune Avenues got filled. Then, all the fire hydrant locations got covered up by those willing to take a chance on a $115.00 ticket. Finally, Surf Avenue was involuntarily reduced to one lane in each direction. There were no parking spaces available as far east as Ocean Parkway. A cement cutout under the elevated became filled with cars. To their credit, the local police precinct did not go on a ticketing spree. Since I was driving as well (from near Sea Gate, thirty blocks from the subway) I had to settle for a spot not far from Brighton Beach – and my (then) girlfriend Nancy and I had to view the fireworks from a distance. The thing was, perhaps ten extra buses and twelve extra subway trains (three per line) could have readily handled this holiday traffic. The trains would have come from those laid up nearby in the Coney Island and Stillwell yards. All that would have been needed is for the three trains from each line to the nearest station that is equipped to turn those trains around. The trains could have run, before the fireworks display, from that yard express to Church Avenue on the 'F', 59th Street/4th Ave. on the 'N', 36th Street/4th Ave. on the 'D' (West End) and Prospect Park on the 'Q' (Brighton). The extra services could then have run between the regular service trains picking up people back up on the way back to Stillwell. From there, these trains could return to the lay-up tracks within the yard upon which they had been resting in the first place. At the conclusion of the fireworks, these same trains could have returned to Stillwell Avenue Coney Island station, making all stops to the above mentioned stations (by then, most of the people would have gotten off) and then these same trains can reverse direction and return empty back to the layup positions in the train yard.

This way, the subway system could have used trains that were not in use anyway. Residents of Brooklyn could have enjoyed the fireworks without having to worry about where to park, or losing that great parking space at the beginning of the evening.

And some employees could have made a few hours of overtime, since those men and women are always around. Years ago, runs such as these were called "Specials", back when people noticed there were enough changes in traffic density to warrant an extra train or two. A similar solution, using the city buses, could have happened even quicker than on the subways. It's just funny how it takes a retired motorman to notice and suggest all of this.

But this is just one example of how constant service disruptions will, over time, make people less dependent on the subway system. Today, (2019) most New Yorkers see the subway system as unreliable, not because there are so many breakdowns, but because the overwhelming number of rcrouted trains and service diversions. New Yorkers will take to the overcrowded streets – made even more restrictive with bike lanes and such – in their cars while there are a number of seats that may go empty on a fully developed and mature transit system. And, they are not likely to return. Don't believe me? Try driving in Brooklyn. Or anywhere else in New York City.

*As a Manhattan Bound, A train leaves the JFK –
Howard Beach Station, newly arrived tourists from
overseas try to ignore the bag lady and her belongings
on the train.*

The Effects of the Homeless People on the Subway

The effects of the hordes of homeless people within the subways are hard to understate. It is worse than most people imagine. It is more than just the smelly guy on the corner of the subway car. The presence of homeless people contributes to delays of people and trains within the system.

I realize that this city is for - and is best enjoyed by – those who are rich, or wealthy, or both. And I realize that a lot of people who are not rich or wealthy are often just one paycheck from homelessness. There were times when I was just one paycheck from oblivion. Through years of sacrifice and enforced thrift, I have done better. Now, I am just two paychecks away from oblivion. However, most working-class people who find themselves on the street don't stay there too long. They are city services that will take them in and take care of them – on a very basic level – but they will be able to survive.

The homeless people that I am referring to are those who reject the city's basic services - often with good reason. The homeless shelters for men are little more than open door jails, full of predators and predation. Many homeless single men prefer the subways over the homeless shelters. And, therein lies the problem.

More than a few – indeed, many homeless people adapt themselves to life within the subway. Those who are weak, or just plain anti-social, allow themselves to become dirty and smelly. The body odor serves as a sort of "protection" that keeps others away. Others are aggressive and threaten the riding public. Still others have an anger that they hold inside, ready to unleash upon the next transit worker that tells them to move, or the first passenger that they think does not deserve to live. A few still try to hold on to a semblance if their prior lives with their shopping carts and bags. After a while, even these possessions get often stolen or destroyed. The homeless often relieve themselves between the subway cars when the trains are idle for a moment at the terminal stations. Once, I seen a track crew, tasked to perform routine work at the old World Trade Center station on the E line nearly "mutiny" because of the smell and presence of urine and fecal material on the tracks.

A small minority of the homeless people are in the subways simply because of bad luck. Then, there are the people who may spend the entire day – or an entire week – without even speaking to anyone else. Some of these people even have jobs - but they simply can't afford a place to live. But most of the subway homeless ended up there because of their own bad choices. These are the people who pee and defecate within the stations and on the platform, and then the trains, and so they seriously degrade the riding experience for the public, and the employees. It often takes multiple calls from transit workers, over a period of weeks, to get one of these persons removed from the trains and sent to a hospital or elsewhere. And there are always "new" homeless people coming down to the subways. I have seen some people go from slightly embarrassed "all night" person who feels that his condition is temporary, to a smelly, repressed bum. The process takes about 6 to 8 months.

The city has what they call a "homeless outreach" program that, in my observation, does exactly nothing. The college kids that this organization sends down to the subways recoil at the first hint of body odor. If body odor does not work, a few well placed curse words will send these kids scurrying out of the subway car.

The police do their level best to avoid the contact at all with the homeless. Their tactics include taking forever to arrive at the scene while hoping that the problem will resolve itself. Or they may take forever at the scene, hoping the homeless will open their eyes and respect the uniform. But, when you look at things from a homeless person's point of view, - why respect the police at all? The meals in jail, if you care to call it that, are free, and they have to feed you.

This leaves the lowly transit worker, usually a conductor or train operator, with the task of "cleaning out" the trains. The usual way of getting the homeless people off, by banging on the seats with a wooden collector shoe paddle while hollering "last stop" often engenders resistance among the homeless, whether by not moving at all, up to angry confrontation. The best way, from my experience, has been to simply tap the homeless person on the shoulder (with gloves on!) while simply stating that the train is a lay-up (short for laying the train up in a yard or storage track). Most of the homeless on the subway understand the words "lay-up" and "last stop".

But the process of "cleaning out" the train is slow, and when one has to repeat this over and over again, with 20 or 30 homeless people on board, the train delays to the riding public on the following trains become excessive. I am not overstating this situation, people.

At some terminals such as Coney Island – Stillwell Avenue 179th Street on the 'F', and especially at

Parsons – Archer on the 'E' line, the riding public will often be delayed 10 to 15 minutes on a following train as the train crew works to remove the homeless people from a train within the terminal station. On the other track is a regularly scheduled train waiting for its' departure time. If you have waited while on an E or a J train at Sutphin Blvd, waiting to get to Parsons/Archer terminal or on a Q or F train at West 8th Street, waiting to get to the Stillwell Avenue/ Coney Island terminal, it is usually because of this homeless person problem. Furthermore, those people who arrive at the latter two terminals will often end up missing a connecting bus to their homes, which increases the frustration factor, exponentially.

And, of course, this problem occurs all over the subway system. I have not mentioned any terminals in the 'A' (formerly IRT) division because I have not worked there and seen the conditions with my own eyes. But I can imagine the same thing going on is such places as Main Street on the '7' line or 242nd Street on the '1' line.

There is no easy solution to the problem of the homeless people within the subway. But it is not a "solution" to have the homeless people staying onboard the trains, either. But New York City houses have an average of 60,000 homeless people each night – the population of Bucks County, PA, Cheyenne, WY or Albany – in Oregon.

Perhaps it is time for the New York City subway to open its own, very basic, homeless shelter. Or, the subway top level supervisors can work with the city to develop a real homeless outreach program.

Of better yet, perhaps it's time for this city's Mayor to recognize that the homeless people within the subways need to be dealt with, that the homeless people as a group are not the subways problem, but the city's problem.

The Effects of the Homeless Upon Myself

Sometimes, the easiest thing that a person can do is to classify and pre judge other people. Living in this manner might make things 'easy', and it gives one a sort of "heads up" on who to avoid, and who not to avoid. To me, living life this way blinds you to those who might do you wrong because, you thought that they were in the "right" group. It also blinds you to those who would do right by you because they are in the "wrong" group.

When you take the time to see each person as an individual, you will eventually find a cross section of society. You will also find that people, at their core, are basically the same. It is because of the many routes that we take in life that we all appear different to one another. And every once in a while, we will find somebody who leaves an indelible impression in our lives.

Such was the case with a homeless person within the subways. Tony Butler was such a person. He stayed within the subways for years. He saw his homelessness not as a handicap but as a kind of freedom. He was easy to talk to and he had developed many strong friendships among the transit workers and subway passengers who he had met. Personally speaking, I remain thankful to Tony Butler. After all, it was through him that I was able to get a very nice temporary job.

In this September 2002 view, Tony Butler, the homeless person on the right, plays a game of chess against a subway conductor at the old Stillwell Avenue – Coney Island station. Tony won that game.

While working within the subways, I first noticed Tony through the many chess games that he had played against other transit workers. He had gained a reputation as someone who was hard to beat. Tony always carried a chessboard and pieces with him, along with his belongings. He never got over confidant about his chess playing and he rarely played for money. Yet, it was easy to converse with him. This fact alone made Tony stand out as most homeless people within the subways seem to be reticent, or dealing with their own personal devils or even occluded. Tony also showed an interest in football and he was able to watch some games from outside of the large crew room at the old Coney Island-Stillwell terminal.

Later on, when I worked the F line, I ended up seeing Tony more often, mainly at the southbound F line platform at the Broadway-Lafayette station in lower Manhattan. Although Tony looked as ruffled and unkempt as any homeless person, he never had to beg or bother anyone. Several people took care of him. Once, a conductor that I was working with had me leave the station slowly in order to pass him a meal. Later on, I had passed to him a magazine I had written about the subways. A few days later, there were the inevitable subway delays on the F line. When I had arrived at the Broadway-Lafayette station, Tony was there. I had a minute or two to converse while the train doors were open. Tony told me that he had started to read the article that I wrote but he was not interested in the trains. "But, I know a dude who is", he confided. With that, he returned to his bundled belongings. It was now time for the train to proceed but I waited anyway. After about a minute, Tony handed me a soiled business card. "Give this dude a call", he said.

That dude turned out to be Steve Zeitlin, who is the director of City Lore, an urban folklore organization. Mr. Zeitlin and his wife Amanda are great people who keep art and poetry alive for many of New York's artistic souls. And, it was Steve who introduced me to Nancy Groce, an officer within the Smithsonian Institution. After meeting Ms. Groce, and showing her my magazine article on the subway, I was invited, along with Sandra Lane, another subway train operator, as co-hosts in the 2001 Smithsonian Festival in Washington DC. This particular festival featured all things New York, down to trucking the body of a subway car down to the Mall in DC. The festival lasted for two weeks in the June and July southern heat. But my time there was one of life's greatest pleasures.

Tony Butler died in 2004. He was memorialized at the City Lore offices on 1st Street. I went there along with a few other transit workers. After we all took turns talking about our experiences with Tony, Steve Zeitlin played a recorded interview of Tony. I had always wondered why Tony choose to live life the way that he did. That interview gave me a clue. "Wrong dominates" Tony said, with conviction. "Wrong is what makes the world go round". It was if as Tony was referring to some force or action that hit him so hard that he did not try to get back up. I felt that his talk about 'wrong' was the talk of someone that had been defeated. After this defeat, it seems that he had simply adapted to this new way of life. As I write this now, the thought of this situation made me stop and think about this. Tony's memorial was covered in the April 20, 2004 issue of the New York Times.

THE CAPITAL PLANS

The Capital Plans

Within this section of the book, I would like to discuss the ongoing building, rehabilitation and infrastructure projects within the MTA. While the focus will be on the subway projects, I cannot ignore one huge LIRR project – the East Side Access, which will be discussed shortly. Still, my plan is to keep this section fairly brief, if only to keep from numbing your minds and infuriating you (if you are a New York taxpayer) at the same time. These were the feelings that I had while I was looking through past, and present MTA Capital Plans over the preceding thirty years.

Billions and billions of dollars have been spent on previous MTA capital plans. The amount that I have found come to a total of 87 billion dollars spent by the MTA for the subways alone in the last 37 years. This amount does not include the projected spending on the upcoming 2020 to 2024 capital plan. The amounts that I have below come from both the MTA itself, online, and the earlier amounts come from the PCAC (Permanent Citizens' Advisory Committee to the MTA).

Capital Plans Years:	1982-1991	....	11,030 billion
	1992-1999	....	12,591
	2000-2009	....	31,217
	2010-2014	....	11,649
	2015-2019	....	14,500
Total (with rounding)........................			86,878 Billion

I cannot certify that the amounts of money shown were exactly the amounts spent. But these amounts shown are definitely in the ball park, like right down the first base line.

Now, I've got to ask you, fellow New Yorker, does the subway look like or feel like the 87 billion dollars that have been spent? Do you think so, while standing in the Chambers street station on the J line?

Don't get me wrong. A whole lot has happened over the last thirty seven years. Two thirds of the subway's 6,000 car fleet has been replaced. Just about every mile of mainline track has been renewed. A few new, but short subway extensions – the 63rd street tunnel, the extension to Parsons/ Archer, and the Second Avenue subway – have been opened. Many stations have been refurbished (and then left to deteriorate once more – think of Bergen Street on the F and G lines in Brooklyn). The total replacement of the Coney Island - Stillwell subway terminal was seen by everyone to be totally necessary. No one misses the old, historic Stillwell terminal. But to me, the investment that I see is not $87 billion. Maybe it is $30 or $40 billion.

There is so much more that needs to be said about the MTA's spending habits of the past, present, and future. The material goes beyond what can be stuffed into a paperback book. I have to keep in mind that I am writing this book on "a deadly subject" (A lady in Manhattan once told me that about the subject of trains and railroading). I don't want to bore you with numbers and blah blah blah. I just want to enlighten you.

In any case, the MTA capital plans have, and will contain brief descriptions for hundreds, and even thousands of projects. Not all of these projects add value to the subway system. These projects add value only to the selected contractors' pockets. Other projects, such as the connecting stairway from the G line to the number 7 line at Court Square are good ideas but totally overbuilt, without regard as to how the facility will be cleaned and maintained into the future. That project took longer to construct than the Empire State Building!

Oversight of many of those MTA construction projects should have been left to competent management. And, they were not. This was the responsibility of the upper MTA management, in particular, the MTA Capital Construction Company. This offshoot of the MTA was considered by most to be composed of "tit jobs", a coarse reference to really easy employment where the hardest part of the workday was simply showing up. It was perhaps a beautiful thing for the few hundred people who were hired to work there. Of course, now the MTACC has been dissolved.

But the present echelon of upper management people are not, on the whole, much better. After all, it was some manager or MTA higher up, maybe even a vice president, that sat down with the contractor or construction company, and listened to their proposal. Someone within the MTA had to non-negotiate with those contractors over the inflated pricing of these projects. Someone within the MTA had to smile and shake hands on that flawed construction proposal. Someone within the MTA had to sign off on the contract that made the sham proposal into a shovel ready project. And, finally, someone within the MTA stood by while that project rose from the contractor's dreams into the taxpayer's reality.

In the following essays, I will pick out just a couple outstanding projects as well as warn you about a couple of projects that are just now getting off the ground (in 2019). Try not to have an adverse reaction........

The East Side Access

Dear reader, if you are not already sitting, then perhaps you should. Let me tell you about a project going on far below the streets of Manhattan. Direct construction has been going on for the last twenty years, although some of the tunnels are about 45 years old. The project is the most expensive in New York State history. The project is the most expensive urban rail project in the world. The project is called the East Side Access. The MTA has paid for this project out of the last five Capital Programs. There is a request within the current Capital Program of nearly 800 million dollars to finish this thing. The total cost of the East Side Access project is 11.2 Billion dollars. There is a long and convoluted history about the East Side Access that I am not going to get into. It is too much to be just an essay within this book. Someone can write a book solely about this project.

Let me just say that the dream of bringing the Long Island railroad to the east side of Manhattan has been a dream of some politicians and transit planners for over 50 years. This dream came much closer to reality when the East River was trenched out and several large tubes, each able to carry four tracks, 2 on top of 2 style, were laid in this trench. The top two tunnels became the Q line to 21st Street-Queensbridge, opened in 1989. Later, connecting tunnels were built between 21st and just west of the 36th street station in Queens. These were connected and now this is the F line. The two tunnels intended for the LIRR below the subway have remained out of use for decades.

Finally, plans came to fruition to build a tunnel from the lower west end of the sunken tubes to a point just under the Metro North tunnels under Park Avenue. The original plan was to tunnel up into Grand Central's lower level and take over about eight tracks there. Officials at the Metro-North railroad did not like this plan although the railroad could absorb the displacement.

Then someone – or a group of people – took the unilateral decision to build, at a cost of billions and billions more dollars, a complete new cavern under Grand Central station. I do not know, but I bet that these people and that decision came from the now defunct MTA Capital Construction company. This cavern will house four tracks, with a wide platform in between two tracks. These tracks will extend to 38th street way underground. A third level will become a wide passenger walkway. Remember, these three levels are below the lower level of Grand Central Station.

The plans are for the Long Island Railroad to run 24 trains per hour (!) in and out of Grand Central. This is close to what the Lexington Avenue Subway runs now. Then, someone decided that all these trains have to go somewhere, so they built a bigger train yard in Port Washington. Do all the East Side workers live in Port Washington? Then, someone decided that an Amtrak train might visit, so they built a connection for them. Then someone decided than a storage yard closer to the station might be a better idea. So now they are building a Midday Storage yard in Sunnyside, Queens. And now someone decided........

Listen, let me just get to the costs of this damn thing,

Over time.....The project was expected to cost – and open up...

$3.5 billion first cost of old (GCT lower level) project

4.3	"	"	in 1999		
5.3	"	"	in 2003		
6.3	"	"	in 2004		
7.2	"	"	in 2008	(To open in)	2009, 2011
8.4	"	"	in 2012		2016
10.8	"	"	in 2014		2018, 2019
12.0	"	"	in 2017		
11.1	"	"	in 2019*		12/2022, 9/2023

*estimate revised downward. Info from Wikipedia.

Seriously now. Will somebody take this mother of all boondoggles on?

OH! There is just one more thing. For the Long Island railroad riders, there ALREADY IS EAST SIDE ACCESS.

It is called taking the train to Hunters Point Ave (I know it's one word but the laptop won't understand). When you get off at Hunterspoint Avenue (there!) follow everybody else, go upstairs and take the no. 7 train to Grand Central. You get there in 20 minutes, tops. It's just as easy as I said it is. Too bad this connection is good only on weekdays.

The Myrtle Avenue Viaduct

On the J and M lines in Brooklyn, there is a junction just east of the Broadway-Myrtle station, where the two lines split apart. This is a very old, flat junction that dates from the dawn of the old Brooklyn elevated lines. Like the equally old East New York yards a few stations east, this old junction was built for 48 and 50 feet long wooden elevated cars. Indeed, the last of the wooden cars ran on the upper section of this line before they were retired, and that line closed, in 1969. Today, only the subway's 60 feet long cars may operate here, and they screech and moan through the tight reverse curves here.

The MTA signed a contract to replace the S-curve – just the S-curve- in this 100+ year old junction. Further up on the M-line, the elevated line, now in Queens and at ground level, crosses over the Long Island Railroad (The New York and Atlantic railroad operates freight trains here but the tracks still belong to the LIRR) These railroad tracks lie in a cut. As part of the contract, the steel girder bridge that carries the M line over the railroad was to be replaced. The new girder bridge is ten feet longer and placed a little higher for better clearance of the freight cars below it.

Personally, I don't have a problem with either of these projects. The bridge over the LIRR could have been placed higher.

What I do have a problem with is the PRICE of this project! The price to replace 310' of elevated trestle and install 65 feet worth of girder bridge is $163 million dollars! This is not a construction contract, this is a contract of theft! I would like to know, WHO in hell within the MTA negotiated this contract? WHAT were they thinking? I'm thinking, that whoever negotiated this contract within the MTA should be FIRED! And not just a plain firing. He or she should fired with a fire breathing dragon in the office! They should come out of the firing office with smoke issuing around the collar, and in blackface!

$163,000,000 divided by 310 feet of trestle and plus a 65 foot bridge comes out to $434,666.66 a FOOT! Divide that amount by 12 and you get $36,222.22 per INCH!

And, just as bad as the price of the project was, so was the time it took to construct the project! It took two whole months to replace the old bridge over the LIRR with the new one. It took 8 months – a whole 8 months – to remove and replace 310 feet worth of S curve girders. And there is no improvement within the new steel structure. The tight S-curve has been perfectly preserved and the M train still hollers on this curve.

On top of that, the MTA's own track department decided to replace the tracks entirely between some of the stations on the M line. That was done AFTER the line was finally reopened in April, 2018. Due to the trackwork, the entire line had to close again. Was it too much to ask the Department of Track to work on the railroad at the same time the line was closed?

Are you perturbed, yet?

Wasting Money Going Forward

The pace of new projects coming out from the MTA family continues, and planning for more goes on and on, into the future. There seems to be no pause, no time taken out to take stock of the situation, no time to say "how are we doing" or "let's look at the financial impact of this project".

For example, a new, recently announced LIRR project that is called the Penn Station East End Gateway will have started by the time you read this book. This East End Gateway will consist of a new and wider stairway and station entrance that will be constructed at the 7th Avenue end of the Penn Station lower concourse. According to online literature provided by amodernli.com and constructiondrive. com, this entrance will provide faster access to both the LIRR and the numbers 1,2, and 3 subway lines. This entrance will be daylighted and it will be marked by a nearly two story high overhang and canopy. Part of the Long Island Railroad ticket office has been demolished, and in this area and just west of this area, passengers will be able to look down through a glass floor to track level. The concourse area will be widened from 30' to 57'. Space will be provided for a number of new stores and retail outlets. The timetable given for this stairway and concourse reconstruction is that the new entrance construction started in June 2019, and this portion is scheduled to finish in December 2020. The reconstruction of the concourse, known as Phase 2, is set to begin in December 2019, and end in March 2022.

My opinion of the artists' renderings of the outside entrance to Penn Station is that the two story high canopy will provide no protection from the weather for people entering the station. The promise of showing the platforms and tracks, along with adjacent TV track information monitors will not change the LIRR commuter's habit of staring at the train announcement boards, and then stampeding towards the train will not change because the current practice of showing the train before showing the track that it is on will not change.

And here is something else to contemplate while we are all waiting for this project to finish. In both press releases, it was said that the Long Island Railroad will pay $170 million of the $600 million estimated cost of the project. New York state will contribute $430 million. Let's think about this, a minute. Isn't the MTA Long Island Railroad a state agency? Or do they think that the public is stupid? Or are we just imagined as such? Why not just say that the state is paying in full for this project?

But, an even larger question is this – why are we paying $600 million for a glorified station entrance, stairway and partial station remodeling?

Let us compare that $600 million cost of modernizing one end of Penn Station with a similar project, way over in France. There is a French proposal afoot to remodel and reconstruct the train station known as Gare du Nord (North Station). For 600 million Euros – at this time (9/19) about 660 million dollars – the French propose to increase the surface area of the station four times, from the present 388,000 square feet to 1.2 million square feet. The project, called "StatioNord" plans to stuff more shops and retail outlets into the station. A fitness trail track is planned for the station's roof (!) as well as parking space for over 2,000 bicycles. This construction is scheduled to start in early 2020 and end in 2024, when Paris hosts the Summer Olympics and the Paralympics Games. This news comes from the September 5, 2019 New York Times. Now, this project might not ever come off as planned. There is a lot of opposition to this project by a diverse array of French special interest groups. On top of that, the French do not have a reputation for fast and efficient construction work.

Yet, in my view, the French promise a lot more for their station than the New Yorkers promise for

Penn Station, at only about a 10% difference in price. The French Gare du Nord is somewhat larger (perhaps 10%..?) in size then Penn Station but it is less efficient than Penn because the tracks at that station in France end at a bumping block instead of running through as in Penn. Curiously, the Gare du Nord serves about 700,000 daily passengers as opposed to Penn Station's 650,000 passengers. Again, this difference is kind of in the ballpark of 10%. Funny how such things, half a world apart, can make you wonder.

The 51.5 Billion Capital Plan

OK, let us go around that this money sucking wheel of fortune once more. In September 2019 the MTA proposed it's spending plans for the years 2020 to 2024. The total for the entire agency comes up to 51.5 billion dollars. The money for this spending plan is to come from several new and nebulous sources, such as 15 billion from congestion pricing, 25 billion from bonds "backed by new (unnamed) revenue streams"; 3 billion that has been asked for by the city but not received yet; the same amount (extra) has been asked for by the state, and roughly 10 billion from the federal government. "The proposed capital program will be truly transformational" says Mr. Janno Lieber, MTA's Chief Development officer. "We have the opportunity to quickly start building the system we need for the future, and through the use of the design-build approach it will enable us to deliver those projects faster, better, and cheaper."

May I offer my translation on that statement? "opportunity to quickly start" = (throw money around), "design-build approach" = (contractor decides what to build or rebuild),

"faster, better and cheaper" = Faster (because more money is available), "Better" = (no, it won't be) "and cheaper" = (and cheaper).

Alright, let us get into the nuts and bolts and the promises made but won't be kept details of this thing.........

Let us begin now with the Second Avenue Subway.

The plan calls for an expenditure of 4.5 billion to "complete" the project. It calls for a terminal at 125th street that connects with the Metro-North station there.

Actually, this project only "completes" the north end. The is still the south end of the Second Avenue subway to consider – far into the future. The planned 125th Street terminal will be like it's LIRR Grand Central cousin, built deep into the earth, below the Lexington Avenue subway. A terminal at 125th Street still does not relieve the overcrowding on the 4 and 6 lines between 125th, 138th and 149th streets in the Bronx. A terminal at 125th street is the work of paper railroaders who do not know how the subway, and this city, breathes. A better terminal would be at 149th Street in the Bronx, where a connection to the 2,4, and 5 trains would bring in riders from three directions. Between me, you, and God, here is a dirty little secret. The 2nd Ave tunnel is already built north to about 116th Street. This tunnel was built back in the 1970's. You can peer back there a little bit from the north end of the 96ᵗʰ Street/2ⁿᵈ Avenue station of Q? M? Or whatever the line is now. We don't need 4.5 billion for 29 blocks – oh, I mean 9 blocks of tunnel.

Signals, including CBTC. 7.1 billion dollars, basically to install CBTC on six lines.

Well, I spent about a fourth of this book commenting on that. We don't need it. Period.

Station Accessibility: 5.2 billion to make 70 stations accessible in accordance with the Americans with Disability Act so that no passenger will be more than two stations away from an accessible station.

I am not against this at all. I just wonder about the cost, and would it be easier to develop some sort of "Transit Wheelchair" that can be pulled up a ramp or onto a bus, instead of an expensive elevator at every third station?

Station Improvements: 4.1 billion to conduct "critical" repairs at 175 stations, including replacement of 78 elevators and 65 escalators.

This will never happen. What will happen is a bunch of stations that will have one or more entrances that will be "boarded up" along with a litany of excuses from contractors and transit officials. I guess that everyone forgot that elevator contract where it was to take ONE YEAR to replace all four elevators at 168th Street on the 1 line. One year. I could do better with Ikea instructions.

New Trains: 6.1 billion for 1900 subway cars. This much subway cars is in excess of what is really needed. There are 230 or so R32, 700 R46 and 40 or so SIRT (Staten Island Rapid Transit) cars that need replacing. The R62 fleet is still strong and needs only a refurbishment. Is there yard space for all these extra cars?

At the end of this Capital Plan, in 2024, there will be excuses after excuse, and the subway won't look much different than it does today, but with more scaffolding and blocked off entrances and exits. A 75 billion Capital plan will be proposed to "Bring the subway into the future", blah, blah, blah. Wait and see.

THE TRACKS OF THE TRAINS

The Tracks of the Trains

Well, OK now. With the following set of essays, I feel that I am going to have to get into the nuts and bolts of the subway system – specifically, the tracks and signals of the New York City subways. Dear reader, I don't want you to get bored, yet I do not want you to skip this section. I feel that I have to take you into the hardware at this time. While I really do not want to discuss the vagaries of the signal systems with the lay person, I feel that I have to. There are those who are taking full advantage of the public ignorance of the subways and they are using that ignorance to over contract and over build at the expense of the taxpayer. And there are those who have successfully hoodwinked half of New York City into believing that the expensive expansion of CBTC (Communications Based Train Control – I'll explain later) is the only way to proceed. Indeed, news writers, reporters and even some transit advocates have parroted this bullshit over and over again, until nearly everybody, including those with the state purse strings, until nearly everybody in the city believes this.

If this CBTC system is so good, so into the future, why aren't they adopting this system in other large and progressive subway systems, such as Tokyo, Berlin and Moscow? Why isn't this system "all the rage" throughout the mass transit world? There is one city that is aggressively installing a type of CBTC. This is Paris, France. The Paris Metro consists mainly of two track lines, and their trains are usually only five cars long. To make up for their short trains, close headways are the norm. To install CBTC on their 7.5 mile Line 4 cost 150 million Euros, or about 165 million dollars. For some reason (greed?) the cost of CBTC installation elsewhere is prohibitive. I have a first cost of 350 million dollars for CBTC on the somewhat longer L line. Cost containment is a part of managing these other, foreign transit systems (but not in New York).

By the way, here is a tidbit that you ought to keep in mind, all throughout this chapter of the book. The East Japan Railway, which runs ultra high speed trains in Japan, is preparing for the 2020 Winter Olympics now, like a progressive railroad should. They believe, that by instituting greater discipline and control at the train platforms where the passengers board, they would be able to run two more trains per hour without any further modifications to the railroad.

A Subway System Signal Primer

Again, I would rather not get into railroad specific terms and verbiage. But I feel that I have to explain these things in order to get you to understand what is really going on with all the talk about the signal systems within the New York Subway. Part of the problem is that certain people within and outside of MTA New York City Transit have been capitalizing on the public's ignorance about the inner workings on the subway's signal system. "We need the CBTC system!" and "This is the only way that the subway will run reliably!" - All at a cost of billions and billions of dollars. Dear reader, this is what a salesperson does. A salesperson works to make you think that you cannot live without the thing that he or she is selling you, regardless of whether this is the truth or not.

Maybe some of you, while you are reading the salesman's spiel in the newspaper, your inner voice will softly say "That is not true" or "We don't really need that". The goal of this essay is to add a little strength to that "inner voice" so that a "We don't really need that" voice can become collectivized and a lot louder. And I will repeat a similar theme within several other essays within this book. I would like you, dear reader, to think of these as hammer blows against a well built up wall of lies and bullshit.

And since this lie of the having to build a complete new subway signal system that will run between 30 and 40 billion dollars of taxpayer money – a lot of money in my eyes – it is important to relate my view. At this time (2019), there are actually three different signal systems within the subway. In order to knock down some of the public ignorance about the signals within the subways, I will give brief descriptions of each.

I'm sorry railfans, but there won't be enough detail here to satisfy your thirst for the subway system info. Please remember, with this book, I am trying to reach and relate to the lay person and general public. So, here goes.....

The 1930's Signal System. In the spirit of working with the truth, I would now like to call this system the Legacy signal system. Legacy, as in meaning, "What was there before". Using the word "legacy" eliminates the negative connotations. Having said that, the legacy signal system is an electro – mechanical (moving parts powered by electricity) system of regulating train traffic. The system operates on a series of fixed electrical "blocks" or wired sections of train track upon which the train operates. This system will communicate to the train operator (not the conductor) the condition of the tracks ahead, whether there is another train up ahead or whether the present train will be switched to another track. These conditions are communicated to the train operator in the form of railroad signals. The signals will display not only the colors of red, yellow, and green, but certain signals will display another combination of these (and other) colors. The train operator has been educated to react to these signals in different ways. This is pretty much the basic way not only of the subways, but of all railroads in the world.

The legacy signal system is rock solid reliable. However, the legacy signal system needs an ongoing program of periodic inspection and maintenance. Over the years, with small improvements such as LED lighting, the system needs much less attention. Doing this work was not a problem "way back then" when a human being was required to inspect not only the signals, but the track as well. Over the years, track inspection has become more automated with track inspection cars. But that legacy signal system still needs that periodic maintenance. In my opinion, keeping up behind the legacy signal system is well worth it.

I would like to add, and I will repeat this again shortly, that the MTA has performed a lot of work with the legacy signal systems. Large numbers of signals and signal hardware have been removed and replaced in kind during the "Master Tower" programs of the 1980's and 1990's where control of the subway rains was consolidated down into several large control towers from hundreds of smaller towers within the system.

The legacy signal system can, in places, support train frequencies of up to 28 trains per hour and direction. (As on the current, pre-CBTC Queens Boulevard E, F, M and R lines).

<u>Automated Train Supervision</u>, or ATS. This system exists only within the former IRT, or numbered lines, with the exception of the No. 7 line, which now has CBTC. The basic premise of this system is that it electronically follows a train as it makes progress along the line. The system sets switches and signals in front of the train, speeding the train's progress, at least in theory. One of the goals of this system was to eliminate a number of dispatcher and tower operator jobs, which it has done. However, this system has to be watched over and maintained by techs and nerds who receive a higher pay than the tower operators that they replaced. The installation of this system from 1998 until about 2008 was long and problematic, with green signals displayed onto tracks with trains on them. The recent meltdown of the 1 thru 6 lines on July 19, 2019 due to the ATS computer failure probably means that this system is aging and other

systemwide breakdowns may be likely. It is more than a little scary that one operating system can paralyze one third of the entire subway system. The story of this breakdown was not as big as it should have been because, in 2019, the subway system is widely viewed as being unreliable, anyway. Can we remind that nerd not to trip over the extension cord next time?

Communications Based Train Control – This system is in use on the L (Canarsie) line and on the 7 (Flushing) line. These two lines were selected for CBTC installation because they have minimal connections to the rest of the subway system. Long ago, back in the 1990's, it was thought that the CBTC installation would not be able to replicate the complexities of the New York City subway. Apparently, those in charge have changed their minds.

The way CBTC operates is that the subway train is again electronically "surrounded" by a block or electronic section. This time, the train is moved by a central computer that controls the operation of train. The train operator simply monitors the system. Since the CBTC system cannot tell when someone is on the tracks, the train operator needs to be there. The trains' conductor opens and closes the doors as on any other train.

The stated advantage of the CBTC system is that the "moving block" that protects the train allows for more trains to run closer together on a given piece of trackage. However, the number of trains that can run on a CBTC equipped line is only marginally more than on the fixed block legacy system. The CBTC system can promise, at the most, about 30 trains per hour per direction. In London, London Transport claims to have run up to 34 or 36 trains per hour. I don't know if this was for each direction. However, even in a 30 train per hour scenario (a train every two minutes) would require a perfectly run railroad, with each train spending exactly the same time at each station, and with NO ONE holding the doors, or otherwise delaying the train.

Now, don't we all know that this would NOT be the New York City subway?

Sometimes, I think that the CBTC technology looks as if it was invented by someone who has never been closer to a train than the Train Simulator software online. What looks good online often does not work out in real life.

Additionally, the CBTC requires the expensive rewire of about 1/3 of the signals on the subway line with the rest to be discarded. A series of transponders must be laid down between the rails. Only those subway cars that are CBTC equipped can run on the new CBTC line, except in limited circumstances. The costs of installing – just the installation – of CBTC can exceed the costs of keeping the legacy signal system and maintaining that for several decades into the future. I have an installation price of 350 million dollars for the L line. It took ten years to put CBTC on that line.

For the 7 line, I have an installation cost of 538 million dollars over a 7 year installation period. Let's not forget – and tally the costs of – the many weekends of service changes or no service at all – on the western end of the 7 line. With the completed installation of CBTC, the number 7 line now runs 29 trains per hour and direction. This "beats" the old number 7 line which ran 27 trains per hour and direction. There is nothing and no one to say that 29 trains per direction and hour couldn't be achieved with the legacy signal system.

Again, the CBTC program also requires nerds and watchers, paid at a higher wage, to oversee the operation.

Finally, there is a high frequency radio communications based train control system within the city subways. But this program is, at this time, just an experiment.

Along the West End line (today's D train) signals were being replaced in-kind, along with tying most of the signal control of the line into one master tower. The newer signal is temporarily hidden behind wood. October, 2000.

Torin Reid photo

The Myth of the One Hundred Year Old Signal System

Within the previous essay, I wanted to stick to just a description of each kind of signal system currently in use on MTA New York City Transit. I did expand and opine a little on the CBTC system. I thought that was necessary. But here in this essay, I will freely share my opinions.

The one thing that rankles me every time I hear it is how the subways are hobbled and held back by the "1930's signal system" or thc "One hundred year old" signal system. Nearly every train delay can be attributed to the ancient and creaking old signal system, full of ancient railway signals that have stood for one hundred years. Listen, people. Listen, dear reader. Stop reading, and listening to bullshit. I will do here what the lazy news reporter or the lazy TV reporter should have done, and gone behind the press release or the running mouth of the MTA contractor, and tell the public the truth. The propagation of lies about the New York City subways signal system is put out there because it makes a better case for replacing the old signal system with the new and expensive CBTC system. The CBTC system, as currently proposed, will take years to install at the cost of billions of dollars. This is detailed elsewhere within the book.

Here is the truth, believe it or not. The CONCEPT of the railroad signal system, with its' series of lights that a train operator must comprehend, is over one hundred years old. And everywhere else in the world, like in Europe and Japan, this ancient signal system is NOT A PROBLEM. By the way, the system of traffic lights in the city streets is just about as old as the railroad system, and this is also not a problem. There is no clamor to replace the traffic lights in the streets, is there? Even if you are in your own self driving Tesla, you will tend to respect the "hundred year old" concept of traffic lights.

Getting back to the subways, now, there are those who parrot the line about the 1930's subway signals. Okay, we have moved up thirty years. But the b.s. is still the same. These signals must also be replaced, because the "1930's" is so old, so outdated, so backwards that today's young New Yorkers cannot even fathom such a thing. After all, one must periodically upgrade their Android, I-phone or laptop every week, right?

Now, let's consider a few dry facts. Not every "1930's" signal dates from the 1930's. In fact, very few are. The drumbeat about the "old" signal systems pointedly ignores the fact that the subway has been working upon the signals since the 1980's. First, there was the consolidations of many signal towers into the Master Tower program of the 1980's and 1990's. There are hundreds of miles of legacy subway signals that date from that time. Most of these signals are in Brooklyn and Manhattan. Then, the MTA began the troublesome installation of the ATS subway system on most of the IRT (1-6 lines) from the 1990's until the first decade of the 2000's. And since that time, the subway has spent a total of 17 years installing CBTC on just two lines, the L and the 7 lines.

Again, listen up people. It may sound as if I am splitting hairs here but in the New York City subway universe, the "1930's" signal system is actually close to the state of the art, for the railroad industry. And it STILL IS. The signal system as installed by the old IND (Independent) lines in the Queens Boulevard lines called for handling up to 28 trains per hour, track and direction. And I doubt that there are any more signals that date from 1930 on the subway mainline. The CBTC as it is being installed on the Queens Boulevard line, at a cost of $900,000,000 will provide for two extra trains per hour on each track and direction. Does this sound anything like a value for money proposition here? There is more on this subject in the upcoming essay "Why CBTC Won't work on the Queens Boulevard Line".

A group of signal maintainers temporarily disabling and the digging out a signal (actually, the mechanical stop arm box between the rails that is associated with every signal) after a snowstorm, on the F line back in the 1990's. Torin Reid photo.

Are They Even Maintaining the Signals?

This is actually a good question. In the back of my mind, I have often wondered why so many train delays are attributed to "signal problems". There are so many signal problems. The MTA often states that there is about 11,500 train signals within the subways. Lately, I have heard that the number is down to 10,800 signals with CBTC now on the No. 7 line. But I have seen that with the ongoing "modernization" of the Queens Boulevard line (E,F,M,R) they do things like replace two older signals with five new ones. So, I am not sure about the current number of signals. This seems like a hell of a lot of signals. But you must keep in mind that they are spread out over 665 mainline miles of track, with additional trackage in the yards. And these signals protect over 700 daily trains. And, yes all of these signals – including those remaining on the CBTC lines – must be periodically inspected and maintained.

Personally, I am not familiar with the job craft of signal maintainer. But, somewhere, there must be a formula for however many signal maintainers are needed to cover a given area. One would think that, for such an important job, there would be a priority made to see that all the signals would get maintained on a regular basis.

But it turns out that the subway has been neglecting this very important – even critical – part of this infrastructure. In a small, one column article that appeared in a corner of the New York Daily News on October 10, 2018, the repair and maintenance of the signal system was called into question.

New York State Controller Thomas DiNapoli's audit of signal work from 2015 through October 31, 2017 says that "Work was pushed off for days." The statement put out by Mr. DiNapoli continues with "Faced with staff shortages, the MTA put off inspections of one of the most critical components of the subway system. (MTA New York City) Transit acknowledges that malfunctioning switches and signals are one of the main causes of train delays. They are badly in need of repair, but it (NYCT) gave short shrift to preventative checks that could save riders aggravation and inconvenience."

The report goes on to state that in two locations, Howard Beach on the A line and at Parkchester on the number 6 line, maintenance, inspection, and testing tasks were done outside of the repair cycle. Of 1,280 tasks scheduled to be performed between 2015 and May 16, 2017, 450 of those tasks were completed late. While most were no more than 10 days late, 83 jobs took longer than 10 days to be finished.

Let us keep in mind that most cleaning and inspection tasks upon a legacy subway signal takes, at most, about a half hour to complete. There were times when I was sitting upon a layup train (a train temporarily not in use) and I have watched the signal maintainers work.

Moving on now, I will again quote from the Daily News article. "Supervisors told the controllers' auditors that they lack resources and that strict safety precautions that have to be enacted before work begins often slow that pace of inspections and repairs".

I am going to put my two cents in on that last quote. First, the safety precautions are not to be questioned by anyone. Second, unlike most crafts that do repairs upon the subway tracks, signal maintainers do not usually require the track flagging people that are normally called out to protect track workers. Signal maintainers usually work in pairs, with one person warning the oncoming trains with restricting lights, and the other person actually performing the work. They work in this manner because sometimes they are called out in emergencies when there is no time to gather up flagging workers.

But, in any case, there you have it. Mr. DiNapoli's report covered just two locations among the hundreds within the subway. There are those that say this report is too small to make a difference. What I say is, that this report just covers the very tip of the iceberg. And while I cannot prove this further (at this time), I have a strong suspicion that the under-maintaining of the legacy signal system, with the resulting train delays, is part of this process to shake more money out of the state for a grossly expensive CBTC computerized subway operation.

Dear reader, please do not get me wrong. I am not in love with the legacy signal system. Nor do I hate the CBTC system, other than the cost and incremental results. Progress will be progress. But it is important to note that other large and complicated transit systems such as those in Tokyo, Berlin and Moscow are not rushing to adapt this technology. And one day, somebody will come up with some kind of technology that is the size of a pack of cigarettes. You will be able to insert this into the cab of a subway car, and the subway car will do backflips! But for now, with a heavy dose of practicality, let us stick with the legacy signal system.

Why CBTC Won't Work on the Queens Blvd. Line – And Elsewhere

Let's move on to another facet of my argument against the expensive installation of the CBTC system. The paper railroaders that proposed the widespread installation of the CBTC in the first place have not looked upon the special characteristics of the New York City Subway. What I mean by this is that the most of the subway lines are interconnected – only the 7 line, the L line and two of the shuttle lines operate independent of the rest of the system. And these lines do have actual track connections to other portions of the system. Not only are there connections all over the New York subway system, there are train yards where trains are stored and repaired, and there are subway terminals that end short of the actual, physical end of the line. So it is with the Queens Boulevard (E,F,M,R) line. Here, the MTA has already spent 900 million dollars installing CBTC – on only part of the line. And that 900 million dollars in taxpayer monies has basically gone to waste. Why do I say this? Here's why:

Roughly two thirds of the way along the line in Queens, as you go from Manhattan to the original terminal at 179th Street and Hillside Avenue, is another terminal. This terminal is at 71st and Continental Avenue in Queens. M and R trains begin and end their runs here. (Although M trains have been making a lot of trips to 96th Street and 2nd Avenue lately). M and R trains headed for Queens and the Continental Avenue station are often backed up getting into that terminal because each train must be physically checked to see that there are no more passengers left within the train before it can either go to the nearby Jamaica train yard or reverse direction underground to begin another trip to Manhattan. In the evening rush hour, trains are often backed up for two or three stations, as far back as Woodhaven Boulevard, trying to get into the that terminal. A lot of time is wasted as homeless people, or even those that are tired, are rousted from the trains. It takes time to wake these people up, and in the case of the homeless, they may resist getting up because all of a sudden, the transit worker is their enemy. And when 3 or 4 platform conductors have to spend 10 or more minutes trying to "clean out" a train, the railroad behind the trouble train backs up. Heads Up! A partial solution to this problem would be to construct a set of switches from the Continental Ave – bound local track to the express track just south of the Continental Avenue Station. But it would take a very good train dispatcher who can oversee the cleaning out of local trains on both sides of the platform without messing up the oncoming express trains. I knew of two dispatchers who worked at

Continental Avenue, who could do this. One person, Mr. G, was male. He worked in the AM's. The other person Ms. S, was female. She worked in the PM's. But I bet that they are both retired by now. And this is just one of the things that the CBTC planners do not see. They never saw the human element. The MTA does not see it either, even though it happens every day, because they approved that 900 million dollar expenditure.

Another characteristic of the Queens Boulevard line is the location of Jamaica yard, north (compass east) of the Continental Ave. Terminal. This yard and shop area has to take in 20 odd – 30 trains each night for the E,F, M and R lines, and then kick these trains out again, cleaned and repaired, the next morning. Each night, trains must "deadhead" (run without passengers) from the terminals at 179th Street and Hillside Avenue (F and a few E trains) and Parsons Archer (E line). These "deadhead" trains must be included in the count of daily trains that run along the local tracks. Why? Because the express tracks in between are being used to store even more trains in the off hours. The CBTC people did not, of course, consider this traffic. If they did, this would offset the higher amount of trains that they promise. On the most eastern part of the Queens Boulevard line, the "deadhead" trains have to be included in the count of trains per hour as they run to and from the terminals. No one within the MTA will tell you this, but I am telling you this. It is part and parcel of why the $900,000,000 dollar investment in CBTC for this area was a waste.

In addition, an act of imbecility was to close the Kew Gardens tower, which handled the deadhead trains from the outlying terminals to the Jamaica yard. Having this control tower separate from the control tower at Continental Avenue not only worked for 80 or so years but it was a tribute to the geniuses who designed the former IND lines.

I was not there at the meetings to green light all of this expensive madness. But I know what did NOT happen. There was no full and direct discussion of the characteristics of the Queens Boulevard line, period.

And, it is not just the Queens Boulevard line that is slated for this madness. And it is not just me who is saying that the CBTC installations would be a waste. There was an article in the Daily News, from October 7, 2019 that concentrated on the CBTC program. MTA spokesman Tim Minton, quoted in the article as saying that only the Lexington Avenue line (4,5, and 6 trains) and the Queens Boulevard lines (E,F, M and R) are two of the only stretches of track where the MTA even comes close to pushing the (current, legacy) signal system to its' limit. The article goes on to say that "low demand" on some lines leads MTA officials to run far fewer trains than the system (again, we're talking about the current, legacy signal system) is capable of handling. As an example, on the G line, the MTA runs only nine trains per hour, despite the fact that the current signals allow for 15 trains per hour. (So, why even bother??) The solution for the G line would be running full length trains on that line, and eliminating OPTO on weekday nights. In my small opinion, the passenger traffic is there, right now, to support this move.

Elsewhere in the Daily News article, the CBTC promises are once again parroted. And once again, no one has taken into account the presence of other train lines, choke points and terminals while they claim all the following improvements.

In the "Modern Signals" the article says, will allow the MTA to run 31 trains per hour on the Lexington Avenue line instead of the current 27 trains. Didn't the nearby Second Avenue Subway take some of the passenger load off of the Lex?

The G train will upgrade from 15 to 18 trains per hour. Why do this if you are only running nine trains per hour?

The 8th Avenue lines (A,C, and E trains) in Manhattan will run 30 trains per hour, up from 24. In Brooklyn, they promise 31 trains per hour, up from 26. I say, what about the fact that the four track subway in Manhattan pinches down to two tracks from Canal Street in Manhattan to cross under the East River to Brooklyn. There, it does not go back to four tracks until after the Hoyt and Schermerhorn street station. What is the capacity at this choke point? 30 or 31 trains? Really? (E trains end their runs at the World Trade Center station in Manhattan). I do not think it is possible to reliably run 30 trains per hour between the above mentioned points, CBTC or not.

Finally, the news article mentions the Astoria Line (N and W) trains. CBTC plans to "improve" this line from 15 trains to 18 trains per hour. Not mentioned is the presence of R trains, which run on the same line as the N and W trains between Lexington Avenue – 59th Street and 59th Street 4th Avenue in Brooklyn (interesting!). In between those two similar sounding stations is the narrowing of the mainline from four tracks to two tracks south of Canal Street. These two tracks continue through lower Manhattan under New York Harbor to Brooklyn. A four track local and express line is not reached again until Atlantic Ave. How many R trains will be permitted to run on this line? Will it coincide with the amount of R trains running on the Queens Boulevard line? And so on and so forth.

Even when these new systems are up – will they stay up? Remember the July 19, 2019 failure of the ATS control system on the numbered lines?

This fantastic CBTC heaven (as they see it) is not fail safe. One incident, which did not make the papers, occurred in October 2014. The ever enterprising subway rat had eaten through the zone controller wiring on the CBTC equipped L line thereby halting all service east of Broadway Junction. They (management) were calling for over time for train operators for several days since then. Later, I had heard that the contractor had installed the cabling using peanut oil. Yes, of course that was smart.

What they are Doing Right With the Track

Not everything that MTA New York City Transit does is wrong or within the narrow confines of some greedy group of people who know nothing about the subways. For once, there is a project afoot which promises to actually help the daily subway rider, in his or her daily commute.

The current (2019) NYC Transit President, Andy Byford, has commissioned a "speed unit" who is tasked with travelling every mile of the subway system in order to find areas where the subway trains could safely move faster. In a December 11, 2018, article in the New York Times, the article states that "207 faulty signals were found, forcing train operators to pass by the signal location at slower speeds (than indicated by the signal)."

The article continues with "But officials kept adding more of them – eventually reaching 2,000 (such signals). Some of them were poorly maintained and mis-configured".

While I am trying to present this as positive, because something is being done about it, this just goes to show you, the reader, about what has happened before this program was started. This reinforces what I wrote earlier in the "Are They Maintaining the Signals" essay.

Still, this is a positive action. Although a New York City subway train is not very fast, at least the perception of speed is important to the passengers' train riding experience.

What I Would Do.

Well, if you have read this far into the book, and you have braved all of the subway and railroad talk about the tracks and the signals, I give you my thanks for that. But at the same time, there is much more that needs to be said within this book.

And I feel that, while detailing all of the waste and mismanagement, I should also write about and detail a path forward. The New York City subway is worthy of an extra intense and more focused path forward because it means more to the city above it than most other transit systems. The boroughs of the city are more or less surrounded by water that separates them from the rest of the world. The subway is important to the city also because moves thousands of people at a time between those boroughs. The subways are, for better or worse, the arteries of the city.

With a huge, complicated system like the New York subway, I feel that it is best to focus upon a few main facts that should be kept in mind whatever one does. Yes, this means "Keep it simple, stupid". Job One, in my opinion, is to direct the focus of the subway from construction and contractors to the most important customer to the subway. And, for the simple price of this book, rather than for a $2 million consultant's fee, I can tell you who is the most important customer is within the subway.

The first and most important group of passengers that ride the subway is the working poor. These are the people who cannot afford to flee to a cab, Lyft or Uber, not even once within a work week. These are the people who suffer through the subways' infamous service diversions with time and money deducted from their timeclocks. These are the people who go to work worrying not just about their jobs, but also about their spouses and minor children whom they had left in bed or with a bowl of cold cereal. These are the people who have left their homes in the predawn darkness who try to get some sleep aboard the trains.

To this end, I would redo the subway schedules and "wake up" the subway system earlier. The rush hour would start at least one hour earlier, at 5am. And the rush hour would last longer, until around 10am. The morning rush hour is, of course, the number one time upon which the subway must do its' job and perform. All of the subway trains that come out of the yard should be on the road by 5am, and not return to the train yards until after 10am. And while the amount of trains can be paired down between rush hours, I believe that the evening rush hour should also start earlier. The evening rush hour should start around 3pm, and should last until about 8pm. And no subway train should go out of service or return to the yards until after 8pm. If this is done on at least a weekday basis, Monday to Friday, New Yorkers would be impressed and they will begin to return to the subway. The overnight hours that are normally used for track repair and construction will have to be moved up one hour to accommodate this plan.

And, you know what? The present, legacy signal system that exists now, can support this level of service. Don't let anybody bullshit you, that it can't. We do not need any more CBTC train control to improve the service.

The next thing that I would do is go before the MTA board and declare that there will be no more contracts let, for anything! No more construction contracts for at least the next six months! I don't care if the next construction contract is for the fucking stairway to heaven! There will be no more contracts let for anything other than work that has a direct connection to improving train service. Why? Because I would want the complete and total focus to be on improving the subway system. And that means getting the trains to run on time, period. And part of getting the trains to run on time is removing some of the impediments towards achieving that end. In other words, I want to get rid of as many service diversions as I can.

After that, I would focus my energy, and the energies of the subway system on getting the legacy signal system properly supported and maintained. Each mile of track within the system would be sectorized and assigned to a supervisor and it would be up to him or her to deploy the personnel to problem areas. And that supervisor will be responsible train delays within his or her assigned areas. This will be the beginning of a more reliable subway system.

Finally, I would insist upon the installation of a heated third rail on most of the outdoor sections of track. And what I mean by a heated third rail is simply the installation of a metal strap that would conduct heat yet be insulated from the third rail. That metal strap would be able to heat the third rail to just above freezing, say about 40 degrees F. This would prevent snow and ice from forming on the third rail. It seems counter intuitive but snow and ice actually interrupts the flow of current on the third rail on the subway track. This makes the subway train stall out, and ruins the service.

Such a strap is not necessary for the running rails upon which the train rolls. The weight of the train will insure the return current electrical contact.

These measures are necessary because, despite climate change, we will still have heavy winters and snow storms in New York City. Besides that, the number two time for the subway to perform is the workday after a major snow or winter storm. After such a storm, many people will want to leave their cars buried in the snow and take a chance on using the subway. A strong performance by the subway system during a snow emergency will win back more than a few New Yorkers. Transit systems in the northern climates, such as those in Canada, Norway and Sweeden, have long been aware of these low tech but effective measures. It's about time that we should be aware of these ideas as well. I will now end this essay here but believe me, I have a lot more ideas behind these, that's for sure.

THE PASSENGERS

The Passengers

The passengers. Ah yes, the passengers. The subway riding public. Yes, let me save the best for almost last. And while I am at it, I am writing about not just any subway passenger, I will be writing about the New York subway passenger, who is the third leg of that distrustful subway triumvirate. I hope that you, the subway passenger, did not think that you were totally without fault.

But it is the subway passenger who is the entire reason for having a subway in the first place, no? I'm sorry, but that statement was the truth. (For my former co-workers who have just recoiled at the previous statement – you can skip to the "Transit Workers' view of the Public" essay). In any case, a subway rider who has been enlightened by this book will most definitely be a better subway rider. The enlightened subway rider will not – or will no longer be – the person that spits and curses at the employees. And it is the subway rider, who is now enlightened, who will benefit the most from this book.

The enlightenment starts with the next essay on the next page. Here, I will begin from the beginning, addressing those people who know little about the subway and its' workings, at least from the train platform. You would be surprised to know who that might be. But before you read too far into these essays, please get yourself a subway map. A Brooklyn subway map, that also shows the city streets is a must for this portion of the book.

The Workers that you are Likely to See Within the Subways

Once, while on vacation out in California, I was riding one of the light rail lines in the San Jose area, checking out how they did things. Don't get me wrong, that was not the only reason I was out there, but I did spend some time on the light rail system. Anyway, I saw a sign that said "How to ride the train". When I read that sign, I burst out laughing. "How stupid can people be out here?", I thought. But, with that sign, the light rail system took out the time to "enlighten" most members of the area's population by printing the signs in Spanish and Vietnamese as well, about the basics of buying tickets and riding the train. After that good belly laugh, I went on about my business.

Over the years, I have thought about that day, from time to time. I have come to realize that most people don't give much thought to using public transit. For most people, using public transit is slightly more complicated than using a public elevator.

The act of paying your fare, and getting yourself to the right platform and then waiting is done without much thought. But now, let us talk about New York. In New York, of course, nothing is as simple as it seems to be. But instead of telling you "how to ride the train" (I still chuckle a little as I write this) I want to tell you a little about the transit workers that you are likely to see when you go onto the subway system. After all, many New Yorkers know little about the transit workers around them (the conductor does not drive the train!), even after years of using the subway. So, let me do what they did out West, and enlighten you. Here is a rundown on the workers you are likely to see within the subway.

The Station Agent – is the person within the token booth (I know, the old name) who refills or sells you a new Metrocard. Sometimes, you can get basic directions from them, or you can get current information about the status of the trains and how they are running. I say sometimes because not all of the booths have a radio scanner or receive information in a timely manner. Some booths seem to depend upon a Stations Department supervisor to get information to them. That said, pay attention to the whiteboard that hangs within most token booths. In some of the larger stations, there are some Station Agents who roam around the station to give info to more people. Many token booths have been removed in the last 10 or so years, having been replaced by machines.

Car Cleaner – This person's job is to clean out arriving trains at a terminal (last stop). The car cleaners are supposed to remove all of the trash and newspapers and, when necessary, blood, vomit, and excrement. It is likely that a subway car containing excrement may be closed up, and the whole train sent to the train yard for a deeper cleaning. This can be a reason for why your train may be delayed later on. This happens more often than you think.

Station Cleaner – This person's job is to clean out the subway stations in much the same manner as the car cleaner does the trains. Before someone says "Why don't they combine these jobs", rest assured that there is enough garbage and effluence out there for both jobs. And you are more likely to see a station cleaner at stations along the subway line rather than at a terminal.

Subway Conductor – HEAR me now! Listen people, get this straight. Read this. The subway conductor does NOT drive the train. Get it right, now. Please understand that the New York City Transit subway conductor does his or her job from the middle or near the middle of the subway train. This person opens and closes the doors the train doors. (Sometimes, some short trains operate with the train operator opening the doors from the front of the train. This usually happens on some midnight runs). But, for most of the trains – 95% of the trains you'll see – it will be the conductor who opens and closes the doors. This job, believe it or not, is actually harder than it looks. After all, they are transporting New Yorkers. The subway conductor is the transit worker that you are most likely to interact with. He or she will try and answer your questions whenever possible, but you should be patient at the train stations. Please understand that there is no training for subway conductors (or anybody else) on how to get where within the transit system. The answer you get to the questions you ask depends upon that conductors' personal knowledge of the subway system. Not all of the subway's conductors are working on the trains. Some conductors are assigned to the platforms on some of the busier stations. These conductors are more likely to have the information you might need.

Train Operator – This is the person who drives the train. Not the conductor. This job used to be called Motorman. 'Nuff said! Normally, you will have little to no contact with the train operator. They are normally locked into the cab at the front of the train. The train operator is responsible for the safe operation of his or her train. It is up to the train operator to correctly interpret the train signals along the line, as well as interact with the train dispatchers and tower operators (who switch the trains from track to track) and then finally, the subway's Control Center (Think "Wizard of Oz").

Train Dispatcher – This subway employee is the one person who actually has the most influence over your subway ride. Yet, you will almost never see this person. The train dispatcher is responsible for overseeing the entire subway line (sometimes more than one line) along with his or her counterpart at the other end. They must react to disruptions and adjust services. This may include turning back trains to the terminal that they started out from. This job can be a lot of pressure at times.

So these are the transit workers that you are most likely to see – or at least be controlled by – during your stay within the subway train. All, except the train dispatchers, wear uniforms. You will be able to tell who is who by the jobs that they do.

Learn the Subways

Once again, in this book. I'm going to begin with a subject that most people think they know, but in fact, most do not know. So, for those of you who ride the subway every day, here is a piece of advice that is tailored especially for you, right now (2019). And that piece of advice is "Learn the Subways, Man!!" or Learn the Subways, Woman!!" What, with the condition of the subways these days, it is imperative that you know more than one way to and from work or school. If you live in an area that has no alternative subway service, then you should look to other means of transportation, such as an express bus, commuter railroad, or even a ferry. Most of the time, another bus or subway combination should be able to work for you. Perhaps you might live close to a Long Island railroad train station that is located within the city. Just pay attention to the fares that you will end up paying on these alternate routes. And, yes, consider Uber or Lyft or even a car service. But using any kind of car service can get very expensive very quickly. The car services should only be used when you are really running late and you really need to be at your destination. Then again, what with all of the weekend, and day and night service changes, you may have been already forced to learn the subways.

"Learn the subways!" I am telling you. This is good advice! In fact, this advice is so good, I am at a loss to explain why no one else has said this before. With this advice, you are certainly getting good value for this book. The MTA certainly isn't telling you to learn the subways. Indeed, I can only think of one other time that someone publicly said "Learn the Subways!" This was in a movie! Yes, in a movie.... called "The Devil's Advocate" (1997). In the movie, a head partner in a big New York law firm, John Milton, played by actor Al Pacino, is in the middle of showing new-fish-lawyer-out-of-the-South Kevin Lomax, played by Keanu Reeves, around the city. "Learn the subways!" Milton commands. "It is the fastest way to get around town!" Did I tell you that the character John Milton eventually turns out to be the devil? Even the devil can be right....once. "Learn the Subways!"

When you are on your way home and going past an occupied token booth, pick up a bus map for your borough. Take the bus map home, and on a day off or when you have some time – the bus maps have everything but you'll have to squint to find it – and you will see that there are many bus lines within your neighborhood and within that borough. Yes, you can use an app on your phone – but try to find everything in that little square of glass. For those of you who are sane, just take the map and unfold it on a large table, with a magnifying glass or some reading glasses. While looking at the map, again, don't forget to consider not only an alternate route, but the express buses, Long Island and Metro North railroads, and even the city's ferry system. Also, don't forget to consider the map when the subway system's incessant train reroutes and planned service changes interfere with your commute.

Another thing to consider is the time that this prospective alternative route will take to get you there. While the express bus will take half again as long as the subway for over twice the price of a one-way ride, a ferry might even beat the time of the train, at the same fare, if you live close enough to a ferry terminal. The Bronx and Rockaway ferries are a boon to those areas.

Most people will find that they live closer to an express bus route. And while this bus is slower and much more expensive than the subway, the express bus is also the safest way to go, by far. Some people are willing to pay a premium for the relative quiet, and the relaxing ride that the express bus offers. People are far more cordial on the express bus to each other and to the bus driver as well. For most people, the express bus might be a good idea every now and then, for coming home on a Friday, a birthday or just after a frazzled day at work.

Let's look at the commuter railroads – LIRR and Metro-North, for a minute. A commuter train is usually the fastest possible means of mass transit into the city. And most of commuter train stations within the city are underused, even now. The number one thing that you have to keep in mind about the commuter train is that this train is for commuters outside the city. Anyone travelling within the city on a commuter train, is frankly, considered a second thought. This means you will have to pay strict attention the railroad time table that is applicable for that station that you choose. If you are not careful, you will watch two or three trains whoosh by before one will stop for you. More than likely, you will not find a seat on this train. If you are leaving the city, pay attention to what stations your train will stop at. There are express commuter trains that go deep into Nassau County or Westchester before they make their first stop. Pay Attention!

Use that info that I gave you above, and that bus map, to plot out an alternative way to work. It's good to have this info in your mind. We all know that in New York, "things happen".

This is all a part of "Learning the Subways". Indeed, this is all part of living within New York City. I can't say this enough. Know your transportation options. When you get up in the morning, tune in to the TV news. Sometimes, they will mention this or that delay or hold up on the subway lines. Of course, not every delay gets reported, And the TV news gets it "right" only about 30% of the time. But that mention on the news of your subway line just might be the "heads up" that you need to switch to your alternate way of going in to the city. Have that second option with you, with departure times, written down on a piece of paper or on your phone, if necessary. This way you can instantly decide if that second option is viable at this time. Learn the Subways!

Learn the Subways – An Example

Well, Ok. In the previous essay, I have pretty much read you the riot act on the subject of learning the subways. So now, let me level it off a little. You don't have to learn all twenty some subway lines and 250+ bus lines. But you should know what you need to do in order to have an alternative way from home to work, and vice versa. However, the more you know about the subways and buses, the better off you will be. So, with this essay, I will take you on a partly fictional train ride from work to home that I have adapted from what I witnessed several years ago. So "hang in there" a little, and read the following example. Doing so just might bring you to a point of view that you have not seen before.

Now, let's take a New York City Subway map, and at least mentally, hang it temporarily, on a wall. Don't use the map on your phone for this. Any old wall will do. The map won't be there for long. Next, let's take a dart. We will throw this dart at the subway map. Bingo! It lands in the Gravesend section of Brooklyn, near the F line. So, for the purposes of this essay, your home station will be Ave. N on the F line. Like most people in a radius of 50 miles around New York City, your work will be in Manhattan. Another toss of that dart, this time aimed at that borough, lands you in your workplace. This time the dart lands near 23rd street and 8th Avenue. So now, you have a 9 to 5 job in Chelsea. Every working day, you'll get up in the morning to take the F train from Avenue N to West 4th Street. Once there, you'll go up two flights of stairs to the 8th Avenue line (A,C and E trains) and you will take a C or E local train two stops to 23rd Street and 8 Avenue. Of course, at the end of the workday, you'll do the same thing in reverse.

So, one day, you are doing the that reverse run, on your way home. You have taken a C train – that train came first – from 23rd Street and 8th Avenue to the West 4th Street. You have come down the stairs to the 6th Avenue line platform where the B, D, and F trains arrive. But, as you turn towards the F line side of the platform, you see that the crowd there is larger than usual. This is not good. Those people who are at the edge of the platform are taking turns peering into the darkness of the tunnel, looking for that F train. Where is it? The platform is warm. Did I tell you that this is the summertime? Normally, this is not a problem as the subway cars are air conditioned. More or less. But the heat and general mugginess on the platform is starting to get to you. And now, the other people on the platform are also starting to get pissed off. Hell, two F trains should have come and gone by now. There was an announcement of some sort, but this was drowned out by an arriving train. In any case, that train was not the one you needed.

Frustration is building, not only within you, but also within everyone else around you. Nobody is saying anything. It's like it's some kind of big secret that the Brooklyn-bound F train is missing. Even worse, your body informs you that, at some point, you must find a bathroom for at least a number one. Not now, but soon. Some people next to you wheel around to look at someone. Over there is a transit employee! There he is, with his reflective vest on. But, unbeknownst to you (unless you have read an earlier essay) and everyone else around you, this transit employee is a station cleaner. Chances are that he knows little more about what was going on than you do. In addition, until recent times, there was a control tower at the south end of the F line platform. At first glance, the place looks like a broom closet. The windows were always covered up.

In any case, a woman calls out to the cleaner - "Excuse me, is there an F train coming?" Everyone within ear shot strains to listen for the answer. Unfortunately, his answer is not what the crowd wants to hear. "I don't know", he says, shrugging her shoulders. As a station cleaner, he is not really concerned with the trains. Since the trains stop at the station only for a moment, he is not tasked with cleaning them. And, he told the truth. He did not know the status of the trains. But the crowd of frustrated subway riders does not see his answer that way.

With that answer, the level of anger within the crowd rises a notch. With that answer, most New Yorkers – maybe the homegrown Brooklynites within the crowd – interpret the cleaner's words as "I don't give a shit". New Yorkers have cornered the market on using and interpreting innocent words or phrases as dismissals or worse. "Have a nice day!" is a common dismissal used by many New Yorkers. It's all in the inflection in one's voice.

Going back to that platform now, all of the passengers saw, at that moment, was a transit worker who at best, was insensitive to their situation. At worst, this was a transit worker who did not give a shit about their situation. At that moment, that transit worker was the representative for all transit workers with the system. And, everybody will remember that incident forever. It's like a restore point in a computer!

Now, that station cleaner may not have been aware of his power – or maybe even an obligation – to partly assuage or even take down the anger and the frustrations of the F line crowd. The station cleaner, seeing the size of the crowd and frustration could have said "I don't know, but I will find out for you" and changed direction and walked over to the control tower and implored the people within to make another announcement. And while we all might say "Damn right, why didn't he do that!!" Well, if we look a little closer at the stations cleaner's own personal work situation – we might discover that the station cleaner was sent on an errand by the station supervisor, and he is trying to avoid having that supervisor say "What took you so long? I just asked you to check on some supplies, and you have to take forever to do that?" And after all, no one on the job will thank him for going to the control tower. The people who run the trains and the people who clean the stations work in two different departments with two different mindsets. Not my department, not my problem.

But what about the control tower? Why didn't they let people know? Well, here is what I have personally seen. If the problem that is stopping the service close enough to that tower, the supervision within may get so wrapped up in trying to solve the problem that they may not think about informing the passengers on the platform. This may sound overly simplistic, and perhaps you might see this as a copout, but it isn't. It's not easy to get control of three or four trains running on the same track when you are overseeing a railroad that might have, at that moment, twenty trains on eight tracks. Plus, one must coordinate with the subway's Control Center, and another switching tower at 34th Street. On top of that, no two supervisors are the same, especially when it comes to handling a stressful situation. And, no two situations are the same. Dear reader, I am just trying to get you to see at least 320 degrees around a common situation – a service delay within the subway. I'll add the rest – the missing 40 degrees – a little later. Right now, I'm going to return you back to that hot, sticky and angry platform. That F train is still missing. The people are ready to riot. Some of these people are now staring at the receding back of the station cleaner. They are collectively wishing that they could cause him to burst into flames. And where is that fucking F train? No one is saying anything, but trust me, these are their thoughts. And as for you, in the midst of all this, on the platform? Remember what your body told you about having to go to the bathroom? Now, your body is asking, "Have you found that bathroom yet?"

But – and there is a big "but" - if you knew the subways – like the devil, and myself, have told you that you should have known the subways – you could have used any of those B and D trains running on the other side of the platform to get you around the problem at West 4th Street. After all, during this whole time, B and D trains have been running like trolleys behind you on the opposite side of the platform. You have been ignoring this because seeing those trains come and go made you even more angry. At that station, and at the location where you live (remember, you live at Ave. N), there are a number of ways you could have done this. For brevity and clarity, I will select just two ways to get you home. If you had just turned around and boarded one of those D trains, you could have taken that D train all the way to Bay Parkway in Brooklyn. After that, getting to your home station (Ave. N, on the F line) will now take some walking. You must also have a sense of direction (or a GPS on your phone). Once you get off at Bay Parkway, you must walk northeast (opposite of the direction of the train you arrived on) to 65th Street. At the intersection of 65th and Bay Parkway, you will make a right, and walk southeast on 65th Street for two blocks, to 24th Avenue. Then, you'll turn left, and walk northeast again on 24th Avenue five blocks to the triangle at 60th street and Ave. N. At this point, the F train line is directly above you, and McDonald Avenue, which runs under the F line elevated structure, is in front of you. You are now very near to where you started this morning. This is all easier than it sounds.

Now, dear reader, I think that I might know what you are thinking. You may be thinking "Why do I have to go through all this crap to get home? The F train should have been running in the first place! Now, I gotta walk all through Brooklyn, from another train, just to get home?"

My reply will be no, you don't have to go through all of that just to get home. If you prefer, you could have stayed on that heated platform at West 4th and continue to be angry, along with everyone else. You could spend your time cursing every transit worker from now on, or plot jihad against the MTA. Your body could force you to flex your bladder muscles to the extreme, after those earlier reminders were ignored. Eventually, an F train will come. But chances are that you won't even be able to board it, because the crowd ahead of you will storm the train as if it was Noah's Ark. You might have to wait two or three trains, just to get a seat.

Or......you can go home with this Plan B way. This is not something that you will have to do every day. You can also say to yourself well, I did something about that delay, and I solved the problem of getting back home. That seesaw walk from the D train station lasted all of about fifteen minutes. You'll get home a little late because the D train takes longer. But, again, you will also have the satisfaction of having solved the problem, and also helping your heart by walking, instead of frying your brains and damaging your heart with anger. You can also reassure your body that you will soon be able to get home to the bathroom instead of holding.....and holding. Even if you detest walking, you could have just taken a cab from Bay Parkway. But the $6 - $8 cost would be wasted money, in my opinion. And, think of the positives – you might discover an interesting store or restaurant along the way. If you had "Plan B" on a piece of paper, or on a phone, that choice to use a D train would have been an easier choice to make.

I had said that there were two ways to get to Ave. N from West 4th in Manhattan. The other choice is to take the B train from that same platform to Prospect Park, and change there for a local Q train. The B and Q trains run parallel to the F line in this part of Brooklyn, roughly fifteen city blocks apart. The closest station in this instance would be Avenue M, and that would be about a 33 minute walk (!). Perhaps it would be best to take a cab! However, be advised that the B train stops running around 9:45 each evening, and is not available on the weekends. But, once again, this is something you won't be doing every day. More importantly, with either route home, you will have learned to "zag" when life in New York gives you a "zig".

Finally, let us go back to West 4th Street on that fateful day once more, so that I can give you that last 40 degrees or perspective. Please remember that this incident happened several years ago, and that some of the infrastructure (but not the routes!) have changed. I'm going to finish elaborating to you about what that control tower was actually doing. The missing piece was as follows. A southbound F train struck someone who was on the tracks at 14th Street. When this happens, it takes from about 20 minutes to around one hour or more to remove the person from the tracks or from under the train. It depends on whether the person is dead or alive. The job of the tower, along with the subways' Control Center, and in this case, another tower at 34th Street, is to establish some kind of substitute service around the problem area. In this case, another F train behind the accident train had to be held in the station at 23rd Street. A third F train has just left 42nd Street, and had to be halted at 34th Street. Now, this is three F trains – 24 minutes' worth (using an 8 minute headway). Unfortunately, the nearest point where the F trains can be switched over to the parallel B and D lines is in between 42nd and 34th Street. That 3rd F train was already over the switches at that point.

Yet, another F train, a 4th one, was coming into the 47th – 50th Street station. This 4th train would end up being the first southbound train into West 4th Street for over a half hour. Keep in mind that the 4th train would have to wait behind the next B or D train to gain access to that trackage, and run express around the other three F trains. That F train will be able to switch back onto the F line just before the West 4th Street station. Please keep in mind that the 4th F train will be the one that you will not able to board due to overcrowding. To coordinate and deal with all these trains via a handheld radio – and I have not even mentioned the uptown trains and the 8th Avenue trains – and you may be able to see that the control tower had a lot on its' hands and no one thought to monitor the elapsed time and make an announcement. Hey, the transit workers are only human, too.

Perhaps all of this talk about trains may be a lot for you, the reader, to take in. Read this essay again, if you are not sure where I am coming from. The main thing is, I have tried to give you a 360 degree look at a subway train delay. And I have also given you an alternative where you can do something about that delay.

A Note about the Subway Car Environment

Again, the great majority of the subway train riders simply want to get wherever they need to go. They do not abuse the subway cars that they ride in. However, there are plenty of people who do, starting with those who sleep upon the long bench seats of the cars. Then, there are those who put their feet (and dirty shoes) up on the standee poles, not caring that the next person to hold that pole might be a small child who cannot reach above where someone had their dirty shoes.

And then there are those who insist upon or who involuntarily leave their vomit, urination, defecation, and blood within the body of the subway car. As I have described earlier, a car cleaner will address these problems at the train's terminal, or last stop. You can tell the car cleaner about a dirty car as well. Just use a little tact, and give that cleaner the number of the subway car that is soiled.

But what about when the train is en route? Well, in these cases, it is incumbent upon you to be just a little more proactive in your thinking. That last open seat might be open because something other than someone's behind was in it. It is up to you to visually inspect the seat and the area before you sit down. I have actually seen a seat where a woman sat, and she was on her period and not wearing any panties or panty liner. The blood shows up as a thin red line on the seat. Just in case if this is news to somebody, this is disgusting! So, this important seat inspection won't take more than a half second. If you lose the seat because you looked, well, so be it. That other person might have a problem.

At this point, I will tell you that it is a great idea to have a pack of tissues, or some alcohol or Handi-wipes with you when you are riding the subway. The goal here is not to perform the cleaner's job, but it is to make you own little space a little safer for yourself, even if the feeling of being safe and clean is only psychological. This advice goes double if you are a mother with children. It would help to wipe all of those surfaces that your child might touch, especially when you are not looking. The standee poles are a prime example.

The good news is that so far, all of the current epidemics and pandemics (ebola, zika, etc.,) are coming via mosquitoes, and unfortunately, sex. If anything came via touching anything in the subways, well, it would have happened already.

Your Safety

Since this whole book is about being in New York, and specifically New York City, I feel that I have to discuss the possibility of crime and the potential of being a victim of crime. (Those of you who are criminals, please skip this essay).

First of all, you who are reading this now, well – you know who you are. If you are a female, you are probably better attuned to the possible actions of others more than I am, a clueless male. Personally speaking, I am used to being one of the larger people within whatever space I am in. Normally, I am not afraid of anyone. As I get older, I feel that I may have to recalculate that mindset. The criminal always looks for what is to him or her the easiest target.

Generally speaking, what happens when a crime is committed on the subway – or really, anywhere else – you are alone. The crime could occur within a crowded subway car or a crowded sidewalk – but for that moment of the robbery, you are alone. It is possible that you could be gravely hurt or killed. People may help you after the fact, but for the most part, they do not want to be part of a robbery or theft, or even part of trying to break up a robbery or theft. Good Samaritans are often hurt or killed within a robbery.

Lately, it seems that young men, for whatever reasons, wish to take out their aggressions upon others who they deem weaker than themselves. They often wait until you are one or two steps past them before they attack you. You can often tell these people apart because they will try and act as if you are not even there. It is as if they are trying to neutralize you in their minds before they neutralize you physically. When you see such a person – you can size him up – c'mon, you are a New Yorker – you know how. If you think that this person is a danger, don't continue to walk in a straight line, but step off to the side, as if you are avoiding dog poop – and watch the shadow of this person. This will give you a slight heads up if this person is actually after you. Again, this advice is as good for the streets as it is for the subway.

The worst of all the crimes are when someone pushes an unsuspecting person into the path of an oncoming train. You will never know that this is happening to you until it happens. To prevent this horrific crime from happening to you, it is imperative that you act like you are holding up the station wall behind you or one of the station pillars that are near the edge of the platform. Do not stand close to the platform edge, even if it means you are going to miss a seat on the arriving train.

Now, I am going to say one more thing about being a potential crime victim in New York. And this is not just for the subways. This is for the streets above, as well.

If you feel that you are likely to be a crime victim, then I believe that you should have an equalizer. I will leave it up to you what you think that an equalizer means to you. I will say what an equalizer means to me. It is something that will change an aggressive person's mind about making you a victim of crime. I do not care if that equalizer is a penknife or a cannon. That decision, I will leave up to you. 'Nuff said.

The Transit Workers' view of the Public

And, yes, there is another point of view that you, the passenger, the subway rider, ought to know. In this essay, I am going to give to you (meaning, the subway rider or passenger) a look at how you are viewed by many, if not most transit workers that you are likely to come in contact with. Yes, this is a chance to see things from the other side.

But first, I would like you to know that the transit worker comes from the same neighborhood as you. He or she is worrying about the same things as you, and he or she often has the same problems as you do. The transit worker is worried about their kids in school as you are, and they fear the next increase in rent as you do. But when they put on that uniform each day and go to work, a lot of things change. The transit worker has to work under a lot of misperceptions. And there is little sense of power in that uniform. The transit worker knows that he or she is not a police officer.

Also, there is one more thing that needs to be said. This is something that is true for all human beings, and not just transit workers. We all, as people, react differently to a negative situation or encounter as we would to a positive situation or encounter. I know that most of you are thinking, "Duhhh", but give me a second here, that's not quite what I mean. What I am saying here is that the negative situation or encounter will have a deeper, and more lasting impact, in our collective minds (by about 10 times, I reckon) than a positive situation or encounter. A "Fuck you" has ten times the mental "weight" of a "Good morning" or a "Good evening". The kicker to this is that a "Good morning" or a "Good evening" is five times more likely to happen than the negative saying, even within the subway. And this is so for both the transit worker and the passenger. Personally speaking, I will always remember the people who (I think) went to the yeshiva at 190th Street on the A line, back when I was driving the train there. Those people almost always managed to say hi or at least gave me a smile.

What I have described above, along with the fact that the transit workers operating your train or bus did not cause the delay or disruption, is something that you, the passenger, should keep in mind whenever you are in the subway. And don't worry, I have addressed the state of the service elsewhere in this book. And I will tell you how the transit worker should see as well, right now. The transit worker has to continually keep in mind that 95% of the riding public simply wants to go from one place to the other, no more, no less. And there is more to that as well.

So now, after saying all of that, I can now say this. After having been on other transit systems around the country, and in Canada and Europe, I can safely say that the New York riding public is the worst, ever! And this was before the current transit meltdown. That 5% of people is a pretty big 5%. I know of no riding public that trashes more, pisses more, shits more, defaces the trains and stations more, and displays antisocial behavior more, than the New York subway passenger. Seriously, people, most other transit riders in the world don't have that percentage of riders that take their anger out on their local transport systems and employees.

And I suspect that, in varying degrees, the LIRR conductor (especially!), the NJT, Amtrak and Metro-North conductor, the intercity bus driver, and even the New York based airline flight attendant, would agree with me!

Many New York City subway employees, especially those in the station agent and conductor titles, arrive on the property as brand new rookies. They arrive on the property with the expectation that they will single handedly change the relationship between themselves and the riding public for the better. There is nothing wrong with this, I am just commenting on the human condition, people are always optimistic in the beginning. But in practice, and depending on one's personality, it takes about 1 ½ to 2 years before all that starting goodwill is turned inward. I know this because once upon a time, I was one of those new people.

A sunny attitude can change a lot faster if you are a subway conductor, and someone spits at you, or slaps and punches you. And just because you don't hear about it in the papers doesn't mean that this behavior didn't happen. It happens all the time.

A few years ago, there was a flurry of newspaper articles about bus drivers who were spat on. While the first few articles focused on the bus drivers and how they felt after those unfortunate incidents, follow up news article took a different tone. These later news articles focused on how those bus drivers were able to take time off because being spat upon was classified as an injury on duty. The time taken off was presented by some newspapers (The New York Post) as a kind of free pass, in order to enrage the public. While this kind of injury on duty may not be the first thing that we think of when someone is injured, we need to think again. While being spat upon may not be perceived as a physical injury, it most certainly is. The spittle might not break the skin but there is always the danger of disease transmission. And being spat upon is certainly a mental injury, sure to change one's perception of the riding public. And, how a bus driver or a conductor or a train operator feels is important when you are driving a bus or operating a train with the lives of your passengers in your hands.

THE EMPLOYEES

The Employees

It might be the epitome of heresy to write about my fellow employees. But this goes exactly to what I had mentioned earlier about each department making music to its' own beat. Plus I got pissed off about these problems many, many times before I retired, and they deserve to be mentioned.

I gave a lot of thought about mentioning you tower operators up in here. Believe you me. I won't forget this one guy in Queensboro master tower when I had to lay up a G train each night out of Court Square (Back when they had R46 cars). Once I had to walk the tracks all the way to Queens Plaza to call control to get ahold of this guy. Night after night.

On the flip side, I knew of a tower operator who worked in the old 34th Street and 6th Avenue tower on the D and F lines. This guy really knew his stuff. Between 34th street and 42nd street, there are enough switches at that location to tie in all four tracks. Back when they had a two car money collection train, he was able to route that train to a certain point on the downtown local track between 42nd and 34th street stations. Upon his order I was able to snake my downtown F train, also on the local track, around the money collection train, briefly on the express track and then back onto the local track.

And that's all I will say about the towers.

Remember the Courtesy?

Once upon a time, not so long ago, there used to be a thing called a "courtesy" among New York railroaders. This word, "courtesy" is defined within the (Google) dictionary as a "polite speech or action, especially when required by convention". Another definition of "courtesy" is this. "Transport which is supplied free of charge to people who are already paying for another service". By this meaning, one is thinking of a courtesy van supplied by the hotel when you arrive at the airport. Now let me modify that, a little. When I am writing about a courtesy, I am talking about the act of letting a person in a similar craft or company ride free on your transportation system.

Years ago, this was not a problem. I will go ahead and say that it was the New York City subway who messed it up for everybody, back in the 1990's. Earlier within this book, I had mentioned a Peter Kalikow who was once the head of the MTA. During his time in office, token booth clerks were directed to order everyone else to "swipe their pass". It got to the point where station supervisors stood outside the gates at busy stations, trying to get other employees to swipe their pass. Also during this time all courtesies were done away with. The idea was that an employee should not enjoy any privilege outside of the job. I can't say if this was a direct policy handed down from Mr. Kalikow. But I can say that this policy shift occurred during his time in office.

As a result of the "swipe your pass" policy, others who had a pass that belonged to other area commuter railroads were then denied entrance into the subway system. At places like Penn Station and Grand Central, those token booth clerks who resisted the change and still allowed Amtrak and Metro-North employees on were harshly disciplined as an example to other employees who might be thinking the same way. And there were other Station department employees who were, frankly, too stupid to know any better.

Of course, with this policy, MTA NYC Transit was directing its' own employees to shoot themselves in the foot. And, again, many station department employees put their big, size thirteen, imported feet out front, ignorant of the fact that some people would like to travel.

Every other railroad system in the city charges more to ride their systems. And every other system stopped giving courtesies to the New York City subway employees as well. And the negative feedback went far beyond the east, since people from all over the country like to visit New York.

Let's fast forward to today. I am skipping over a little history but subway employees are once again allowed to ride the commuter trains, with specially marked passes. While that is good, one note don't make no song, B!

Now, the token booths with live people in them have been removed from perhaps more than half the stations. People sneak onto the trains in droves, in certain stations. Sometimes they look like gazelles hopping on the African plain. That is not our problem as employees. That is a managers' problem. What I am saying here is that a Metro North or a Long Island Railroad employee should be allowed to ride our subway trains with no problems. They are us and we are them. So should a New Jersey Transit or an Amtrak employee. So should an MBTA (Boston) or a CTA (Chicago) transit employee. And so on.

And no, I am not trying to propose a kind of transit worker anarchy within New York. Think about this. Just about every airline employee can fly on a space available basis on every other airline (on the for-profit airlines, no less) to anywhere on the planet that a plane can reach.

The Trackworkers

I would like to tell you about an entire class of transit workers that most of you usually never see. These are those workers who work in and around the tracks within the subway system. Sometimes, if you happen to be in the first car of a subway train in the evening hours, you might notice a crew of large men with heavy tools who will arrange to get dropped off in the sooty darkness of the tunnel. It is more likely that you were in another car or the train, wondering why the train had stopped in the first place.

Anyway, these men (and, to date, a few women) are there to perform work on all parts of the tunnel. Now I've used the word "Trackworkers" and that may make you think only of those who work on the track. But I am also talking about signal maintainers, power maintainers (third rail and the connections thereof) infrastructure people and others who have business down there. And I don't have anything against these people or the jobs that they perform.

But I do have a problem when they take over the fucking tracks for miles at a time! I will never forget a trip on an E train that took exactly twice the scheduled 42 minutes to get from the World Trade Center station to Parsons/Archer in Queens.

It looked like there was a party on the tracks down there, all the way to Queens! There were three work zones, one after another. Each zone must be traversed at 10 mph, no more. There were a new set of red lamps three feet after the last green lamp. It's like, collectively, they don't give a damn while the train operator and conductor on several trains lose their lunch hour and break time between runs. Within the whole run that night, there were 17 work gangs.

What this really was – this was a failure of management. One of those long forgotten rules, back when Service Delivery was called Rapid Transit Operations, and had balls, was that only 2 work gangs were allowed on the tracks in each borough. The Foreman of the gang had to call the Control Center to get permission to perform work on the tracks. A TSS told me this. But they relaxed these rules after it was shown that the train operators were still arriving on time at the terminals. In this way, the train operators kind of "cut their own throats" by continuing to be on time. More and more work gangs started coming down. Now – or at least when I retired in 2016 – it's a party down there on many nights. This is just one of the ways that a train can be delayed that the MTA doesn't track.

The Car Equipment Road Car Inspector

If you are a train operator within the New York City Subways, after a certain length of time, you might encounter a operational problem with the train. It might be a major one like a loss of power in one or all of the cars or it might be a minor one like a loose cab window latch. After you make your problem known to others within the system via the train radio, eventually, a subway Road Car Inspector will show up. Sometimes, he (or a very few she's) will show up at the next major station. Sometimes they won't show up until the last stop, when you do not need them anymore.

On paper, and for those who don't know any better, the job of the Road Car Inspector is to keep the fleet of 6,300 or so subway cars in top running condition so that train delays due to mechanical causes can be minimized.

In reality, the job of the Road Car Inspector is to act as a lawyer for the subway's Car Equipment Department. Their singular goal is to try and make sure the any blame for the trains' mechanical condition rests upon the train operator and conductor, and not anyone in Car Equipment.

Well, there's one thing that I can say, and that is the MTA is not alone in this silly worker vs. worker dogfight. Bus drivers and airline pilots will know what I am talking about.

This all stems from the fact that the MTA, along with other transit agencies, etc., have their workers assigned to different departments. The different departments concentrate on different aspects of running the transit system. The train operator and conductor belong to the Service Delivery department. Service Delivery basically sets the train schedules and runs the trains. The Road Car Inspectors belong to the Car Equipment department. Car Equipment, at least within the MTA, "owns" the equipment and does the repairs within the subway car repair shops throughout the system.

So far, the layman reader might find all of this just a little nonsensical. So, let me add this. The MTA has what is known as a system of "charges" in which any incident that delays a train is charged, or blame apportioned, to the department that was found to have caused the delay. For example, if a train is unable to proceed in service, the charge, or "fault" belongs to Car Equipment". If the train strikes a piece of debris on the track, the fault belongs to the Track department. If the train operator's hand slips off of the controller, then the charge belongs to Service Delivery.

Needless to say, there is a fair amount of chicanery whenever it comes to determining whose department is at fault.

Representatives from each department can get into arguments about who did what and what happened when. Unfortunately, Service Delivery seems to be weakest in this area and Car Equipment plays this silly game to the max. Their employees, namely, the Road Car Inspectors, are shot through with suspicion about train operators and conductors. It's as if they are trained to be that way. Frankly, I think that they are.

In the last few years of my working life, I spent some time at Lefferts Boulevard in South Ozone Park on the A line. The Road Car Inspector who was assigned there was quite a character. He spent most of his time holed up in a little office near the fare entrance area. In the event that he was forced from his office on a call, he often patrolled the platform with a tightly drawn face. He was a tall person, and he took advantage of his height by never really looking at anyone. He preferred to keep his eyes on a faraway point, maybe Mount Everest. Somehow, he was the only one I knew who was able to keep his eyes on that mountain from the vantage point of the South Ozone Park elevated station. Should he be forced to talk with someone, he spoke with a whisper in the hopes that a listener would miss something important. Needless to say, he was a master at writing up a report that would shift the blame to the unsuspecting conductor or train operator. Like many Road Car Inspectors, he swore that the subway trains were in perfect condition all the time. Meanwhile, all that the train operators and conductors wanted to do was to complete their trips and get home. MTA people in other departments do not seem to want to understand that. And, once again, this is what I mean when I mentioned in the introduction that the MTA departments often do not work together and they make music to their own beat.

In any case, this particular RCI had to be taken down a peg or two. And I was glad to be a part of that.

And that was not the whole story at the Lefferts Boulevard train station. At night, a couple of A trains were broken up and made into shorter S shuttle trains for the overnight. In the early morning, the shuttle trains would again be made into A trains for the trip to uptown Manhattan. On most mornings an RCI from the nearby Pitkin yard would come over and supervise the operation. While working overtime some nights I encountered an RCI who felt that he had to call the shots on everything I did to couple up the trains and get them ready for the morning rush. It got to the point where he was slowing me down because I had to justify every move that I made, and that began to piss me off. So, I asked him about the lighted side signs on the R46 subway car that were often faulty. Indeed, there was one right in front of us. The side signs would sometimes say that the train was going to Far Rockaway when the signs were actually programmed for Lefferts Boulevard. This fault alone would piss some passengers off and make the train's conductor a target for assault. But this RCI didn't worry about that. He simply said that it would be taken care of after the train's day of service. I told him that he should fix it now. That made him disappear.

Pitkin Yard in Brooklyn maintains much of the R46 subway car fleet at this time. The Car Equipment department there does whatever they can to take care of themselves. For example, they maintain the maximum temperature of the R46 car at 56 degrees – so that they will never have to change a heating element in the car body. And the A line passengers wonder why the trains are so cold in the wintertime.

On the flip side, there are RCI's who do not see other transit workers as the enemy. One memorable RCI who showed up at Lefferts Boulevard actually took the time to show me how to reset those side signs using the circuit breakers inside the subway car. And on another day while I was on the road with an F train at West 4th Street, one young, new RCI actually had an assortment of small screws that he had in a pouch. He actually fixed that window latch that was such a pain in the behind that day on the F train. I was eternally grateful to this guy. But I bet the Car Equipment department sent him somewhere for retraining.

The Union

There are several large unions within the MTA. The union of all subway and most bus drivers is the Local 100 of the Transport Workers' Union. As with my essays about the transit management, I won't get into the personalities that make up the present union. In any case, the present crop of personalities are not as colorful as those of the recent past. What I will do here is offer a dispassionate view on what is going on now, especially with RTO (sorry, I mean Service Delivery) employees. For now, let us set aside the current (2019) contract negotiations.

I look at the current membership, and I see a group of people who do not really expect much from their union and even less from the transit leadership. Yes, I am from that very old school where the leadership took part in leading the employees and not damning them. Many of the current transit workers have come up to transit from even worse delivery and other sounds-great-but-they-kill-you jobs like office or restaurant manager. Now that they are in transit, they say to themselves "Is this all that there is? Am I really going to do this for the next 20-25 years?" Unfortunately, the answer is yes, because the spouse and the kids do not really understand anything else. I sense that the today's transit workers have the same sense of distrust and even contempt for both the union and management that we had a few years back. And as we all know the management, other than Mr. Byford, doesn't really care. The TWU union might care, but frankly, their voice is too small. It seems to me that there are just enough membership meetings, just enough forced outrage, and just enough effort to reach the public so that they can call themselves a union. From time to time, there are voices who rise up and try to be what the union leaders should be, at least within their crafts. But these single individuals soon find out they can't please everybody, and they burn out. And what should that union leader be?

First of all, that union leader should be a unifier. He or she should be able to pull all of the crafts closer together and there should be those in the field who can communicate in both directions. And that should be the only layer of personnel between the worker and the union leader. And of course, all of this is not going to rise up out of thin air. This kind of union should be built up over time.

So, where do we start? We can start be educating every incoming worker about the history and he place in society that the American union had. And about how it is more important than ever it is to be in a union. We have to fight against the stereotypes of the union that the public has. We have to remind the public where the five-day week and the paid holiday comes from.

The current impasse within the contract negotiations of 2019 are there because this is the only way that the MTA knows how to handle it. They are still using the 20 years old playbook. Back then, the MTA management enlisted the help of a union busting firm, Preskauer Rose, to try and derail the unions' demands. Part of the idiot things that they did was to enter into an early negotiation meeting with empty briefcases in order to create false pressure upon the union.

Lately, the management said that they will not negotiate a contract in the press.

If it were me in the union, I would negotiate in the press! I would call a press conference and highlight every negative proposal that the management put forth. I would explain my (our) position clearly, and to the lay person. I would call a press conference nearly every day.

If I were in the union I would highlight the mismanagement and waste that is endemic within the MTA. I would hire a full-time researcher who would find out just how those billions were wasted. And the first place that I would direct that researcher to is this book!

Wither a Promotion?

There I was, enjoying a hard-earned vacation in November, 2015. This particular vacation week was during the week of Thanksgiving, when everyone seems to be on the run to somewhere else. Others, who have to remain at work during this holiday week, are often bummed about having to be at work. I have felt the holiday blues many times before. I remember having to ring in the New Years' holiday on an N train just south of the 59th Street and 4th Avenue station in Brooklyn, After enduring that slow climb up the seniority ladder, I was more than content to let someone else do that now.

So, while I was in that state of relaxation, the phone rang. I answered the phone without looking to see who it was. To my surprise, it was the subway's own crew office. Normally, any communication from the subway's crew office is generally negative. I thought, oh Lord, what did I do now?

And it was kind of a secondary surprise when I realized that this new message was not negative, at least on the face of it. The bored voice on the other end stated that I was now promoted to the title of Train Service Supervisor, effective the following Sunday (which is the first day of the transit work week). For those who do not know, a Train Service

Supervisor is the person who oversees the conduct and the operations of the subway trains' conductors and train operators as well as the tower operators and, at times, even the train dispatchers.

I could not believe this message. Seriously, I could not believe this message. Maybe the crew office representative had mis-dialed. Maybe they were joking. But no one was laughing. I began to dismiss that call as a mistake, that I would straighten out once I got back to work. But, the crew office called again the next day. This time, I was prepared. And so I told the voice on the other end "You got to be kidding me!. His retort was "Well, you took the test!" This was true, but that was several years ago, indeed for me, a lifetime ago, when I had a fit of optimism about the job. My gut reaction was to turn down this offer, and so I told that to the voice on the other end of the line. The voice said, well, that's fine, just write that down as a statement and send it to the crew office. But as of now, he continued, I had the upcoming Sunday off, and that I had to report to the Subways Learning Center (a repurposed junior high school in Brooklyn) at 7 am on Monday.

I was lost in thought about this promotion for the rest of the day. As far as the job was concerned, well, I had one more year until I was eligible to retire. What in the hell was I going to do with a promotion with only about a year left on the job? More importantly, why was I being promoted? In a couple of areas, I had fallen short of what they required out of me for the job. Did someone ignore those things?

Now I remember, back in the dim past, when I might have had illusions about making things better within the subways, but those thoughts had died out long ago. I had seen other people, who had potential, move into supervisory positions within the subway. Either they had slowly burned out to the point where they were glad to retire, or their professional or even their total reputations were ruined by one single incident. And, that one single incident was usually not of their own making.

At the time I had settled into a switching (putting away trains for the night) job at Lefferts on the A line. There, I had sensed that I was doing a pretty good job, as far as local supervision is concerned. At times, I was even helping some of the more inexperienced dispatchers in running the terminal. Doing this, of course, was way out of my title but most people appreciated what I did. I wondered, had some "higher up" person volunteered me for this new position? Or was I just the next list number to come up?

I was just the next list number to come up.

In the end, I had decided not to forclose upon the idea of becoming a Train Service Supervisor. And the idea of having the upcoming Sunday off, which was normally a workday for me, was appealing.

The flip side of having that extra day off was that I had to change my whole lifestyle, and in short order. For years, I preferred to work in the PM hours. This was comfortable to me. In my opinion, working those hours was the closest thing to retirement that a working person can get to. There were no alarm clocks for me. I stayed up late all the time. Late night writing was and is the best for me, when all the world is more or less silent. I went to sleep naturally and I woke up naturally. Even now, I am writing this at 3:25 am.

I realize that most people can adjust to different working hours within a few days – a week at the most. Not me. It took me weeks to adjust to this new life. I guess that this is one of my weaknesses. And everything that is associated with going to work in the morning, I hated. For example, going to the Learning Center in Brooklyn from where I lived in Queens required some cutthroat driving on the Belt Parkway. I knew that I had to be where the Van Wyck expressway exit to the Belt crosses on to the

Conduit no later than 6:15 am if I was to be on time at 7 am. Then, I – along with the other working class lemmings – had to drive that Belt Parkway at 75 mph, five feet behind the car in front of me, and with the next clown five feet behind me, all at (hopefully) the same speed. And this was all before the recent improvements in the road. Back then, the Belt Parkway still had the old drawbridges where the cars jumped up, Dukes of Hazard style, over the short steel drawbridge roadway. Each time I did that, I had to pray that the traffic in front of me was not at a dead stop. After all, the car's brakes don't really work when the tires are in the air!

Needless to say, in this driving environment, I could not take my eyes off the road for one second – most times I could not even tune the damn radio! Then later, while sitting in class contemplating that high speed near miss or that sudden panic slow down, I would miss important facts that might be on a test. I vowed to hang a religious cross on the rear view mirror. Unfortunately, I never got around to doing that. You might think that I am spending too much time on having to go to work early in the morning (Everybody else does this!) but for me personally, this was my worst problem during the entire class. There were many days when I had little to no sleep, and it showed. The simplest facts about the trains, tracks and signals bounced in, and then out, of my head.

One day, we were all in one of the classrooms. The interior of the school looks exactly like how you might remember a New York City junior high school classroom. The only difference was that the fixed chairs and desks have been removed, in deference to all the middle aged pot bellies around. So, we were sitting there, and for some reason, there was no one around to teach us whatever they wanted to teach us. So, one of the (I'm guessing, the deputy director) of the school stepped in for the time being. This man wore a three piece suit, all buttoned down to the max, nearly every day that I saw him. Once he was inside the classroom as a substitute teacher, he kept the class nailed down for about 90 minutes, with a display of subway car knowledge, facts and trivia that I had never seen before. And all of this knowledge came straight out of his head. He had no textbook. He had no notes. He had no worksheet. And he was totally comfortable keeping the entire class on its' mental heels, wondering what the hell would come next. I began to wonder, what the fuck was he doing here? Why wasn't he downtown, running the entire subway system from there?

Later on, a revelation came to me when the director of the entire Learning Center came into the classroom. He was there to address, I mean harangue the class with his thoughts. If you remember the movie film "The Taking of Pelham One Two Three" — the original 1974 movie, not the crappy remakes – There was a supervisor in that movie called Caz Dolowicz who ended up getting shot and killed. This director of the Learning Center was just like him, or he could have been that actor's son. Anyway, the director was there to share his thoughts. Apparently, a supervisor wasn't a supervisor until he breathed fire and brimstone. Subordinates were to walk in abject fear of the supervisor. He warned us with "Listen! You'd better perform, or else!". And a supervisor, specifically a Train Service Supervisor, was to know every aspect of this job. He gave an example. A subway train had broken down on the number 4 line. He had ordered a TSS to "pick up a power pack" (two work train diesel locomotives, connected on either end of a rider car) from a nearby train yard. The TSS was to take the power pack up to the 4 line to shove the offending train out of the way. Unfortunately, that TSS was not up to the task. "I tell you right now, he's a TSS no more!" he bellowed. Needless to say, this man needed no notes for that. His clothing of choice was a double-breasted suit and tie, and sometimes, an unlit cigar.

Both of these directors were prone to walking the halls of the school in their three piece – and double-breasted suited glory, and catching a non-observant teacher or an errant student at fault.

But the most important classroom revelation came to me when a representative for the union of supervisors had the run of the classroom. During his talk, he ran down several small benefits that the union had for its' members. He also took the time to explain that the union had people on call who would represent a supervisor should he or she get in trouble. But it was his explanation of the pay scales and wages that really made me sit up and take notice. Although the full yearly income for a TSS exceeded the yearly income for a train operator, a starting TSS made only 75% of the full TSS salary in the first year. That level of pay would drop him below the salary of a train operator. The TSS salary would increase 5 percent each year until the salary level was fully at 100 percent. Nevertheless, the TSS would have to work about three years, until his or her salary was at 85%, when they would match the salary that they formerly made as a train operator. Thus, all of us were submitting to a three year pay cut. This revelation became a significant personal drag upon my willingness to finish the Train Service Supervisors' class.

At the same time, there were significant advantages to being in the Train Service Supervisors' class. We went all over the subway system, which was a pain in the ass to most of my classmates but I secretly enjoyed this. I liked seeing parts of the A division (old name = IRT) trains and yards close up. Sometimes, I even brought my camera with me. But getting a good night's sleep remained a problem for me. I won't forget the day when I decided not to put on long johns and a sweater because I might get sleepy. Then, that morning, we spent 90 minutes outside, in the 23 degrees cold weather, discussing the one spring switch within Concourse Yard.

As a small defense against those sleepless nights, I began taking the train to some of the different places that we visited. Using the train took longer to get there, but at least I would get to nap for a little while. Doing this was a big help during the day. While using the subway to get to the next assignment, I would run into some other TSS that I had known before I went to this class. There was one man, whose judgement I trusted. I asked him about some of the things that I had heard about in the classroom. I related to this man the episode in which the schools' director was hollering about the "power pack". He told me that he would not let the supervisor know that he had the knowledge to move those diesel locomotives. I was a little taken aback by that. I had known this man for several years. This man had solid, workable ideas about improving the transit system, especially within the Queens (E,F,M,R) corridor. But this man felt that he did not want to share his ideas with any of the higher ups. It seemed to me that this man's personal way forward was to be as quiet and as out of the way as possible. I wondered what had happened to make him think that way. Did someone shoot down his ideas? What did he witness? I did not think that any of the superintendents in Queens were "off the hook" (crazy).

But in my view, the way this guy felt, along with the pay cut, began to form some personal dark storm clouds over this new supervisor horizon that I was facing. I began to take mental stock of the other TSS that I had known in the past. Most did their jobs, simply because they had to. A couple of them did their jobs just because they wanted to fuck with other people. Most took a more or less a middle of the road attitude about things. If you don't mess with me, I won't mess with you. Very few seemed to be happy, or at least satisfied with their jobs, or in the position that their jobs left them. I began to wonder what difference I could make.

I had a year before I could retire. Most of my classmates had a minimum of 5 to 6 years before they were eligible to retire. They had their priorities.

Mine were beginning to change. That retirement carrot was growing ever larger.

But leaving the class had its' own drawbacks. I would not get my original job back, not for a while. I would end up working what they call "Extra extra" in which I could be sent to any corner of the subway system to work, just for that day. A classmate took me aside and warned me of that foreboding fate. I did not tell him that I had once worked for Amtrak as a snack bar car attendant. "Extra extra" on that railroad meant that you could be sent to Montreal or Chicago on a two day or a three day trip.

In the end, I had decided that I would leave the title soon after I had graduated from the class. I did end up going extra extra although I saw this as a farewell tour, not a hardship. The retirement carrot was just too alluring, too juicy. Hopefully, with this book, maybe I could make some changes for the better.

THE REST OF THE RAILROAD WORLD IN NYC

The Rest of the Railroad World in NYC

You know, I just figured, while we are here, on this long, long train of thought, that we should take a look at some of the other railroads around here in this city. The New York City subway does not operate all by itself. I will try to mention them all except for the PATH (Port Authority Trans Hudson) and the freight railroads such as CSX and NS. The freight railroads are not relevant to this book (or it's intended readers) and I simply do not know enough about the PATH system to write at length about it. However, the Port Authority of New York and New Jersey, which is the owner of the PATH system, wastes a hell of a lot of money – at least on a par with the MTA. The Port Authority should have been able to finance the construction of the new Penn Station tunnels alone, without federal help. That is my belief. But I cannot prove this.

And then, there are some other things – like the media –that deserve our attention.

Long Island Railroad

From my point of view, it seems to me that the LIRR is more active than the Metro-North when it comes to participating in the huge capital projects put forth by the MTA. The LIRR capital plan projects range from the East Side Access boondoggle to the fairly necessary third track in western Nassau County. When you throw in several other infrastructure programs, the Long Island railroad is a busy – and disruptive place on the weekends. However, the LIRR is using a different approach than the subway system by backing off on work for the fall and winter holiday season.

The third track project involves a lot more than just adding a third track through the mature suburbs that have built right up to the edge of the present mainline, in many cases. And although the complete project is supposed to extend from Floral Park to Hicksville, most of the construction is taking place east of Mineola. The right of way has received several third track bridges over town streets. Several railroad crossings have been eliminated. On the elevated right of way between Floral Park and New Hyde Park, and additional walls (well, not the one put forth by Trump) that will go atop the present wall to keep the noise of the trains down. And what I described above are just the opening acts.

The LIRR President came to the railroad from a career in highway construction. This means that he is going to keep going after those infrastructure projects, and weekend delays and reroutes will continue into the foreseeable future. In my opinion, there are other issues within the LIRR that need attention. One of these is the overabundance of manager positions. An observer told me that there is one chief for every three Indians out on this railroad. Some of the manager jobs have veered from the sublime into the ridiculous. For example, there is the job known as the "Slip-slide Coordinator". Okay, let me explain. On the LIRR (as well as most other railroads) a "slip-slide" condition exists when the rails are covered with fallen leaves, usually in the fall season. The weight of the trains usually crushes the leaves into a slippery oil which negatively affects how the train brakes work. This sole job of the Slip-slide Coordinator is to wait for a phone call from the trains' crew after one of these incidents have been reported to the trains' dispatcher. Two things here....why can't the train dispatcher simply make a note of what happened? And what does the slip-slide coordinator do in the other three seasons of the year?

Then, there is the transportation manager. One of their tasks is to assist with the trains' pre departure checks made on every LIRR train. Essentially, the transportation managers fall into two groups. One set of TM's actively helps with the train pre departure checks. The other set of TM's watches the train crew perform the pre departure checks.

I have heard and read a lot of comments about the LIRR pay levels and their labor contracts. Well, let me say this. Long Island (meaning Nassau and Suffolk counties) is a terribly expensive place to live, not much different than, say, San Francisco. I know of a subway train operator who lives in Nassau County. He is a single man and he bought a house. He has had to have not one, but two people renting rooms in that house with him just to stay afloat. I knew of another subway train operator who had a house by himself in Nassau County. He survives by using as little heat as possible – keeping the house just above freezing in the winter.

Depending upon the craft, some of the provisions within their contracts are actually penalties for the implied misuse or overuse of an employee. Some of these penalties can be as much as a day's pay. This is how an employee can actually get paid for more hours than he has worked. Every now and then, an employee gives up his or her social life and artfully games the system. The employee then retires after years of doing this, and it becomes front page news for some newspapers.

But the important thing to remember is that the employee that did this, did not do it alone. He did this with the full cooperation of his supervisors. In fact, the LIRR supervisors are, in fact, the co-conspirators of that man's fat assed pension.

Newspapers like the New York Post should keep this in mind when they send out a reporter to that man's house.

Metro North Railroad

This particular essay is going to be short. I do not know enough about the Metro-North railroad much beyond the enthusiast stage. As far as the trains go, the service seems to be pretty good, and the railroad is well used. But from what I have been able to see on a closer level has not been all that good.

The New Haven line has been under reconstruction since forever. And I hear that the contractors won't be through with that line until the year 2037. Of course, at that time, they will have to start all over again. Perhaps they could have asked for some advice from the original New Haven railroad, which electrified and built out the railroad from New York to New Haven, Ct. They basically built the four track line that you see today – in 1914, after only ten years of reconstruction. In contrast to the Long Island railroad, there are many small bridges that have been replaced but the road clearances have not been enlarged or changed. I saw this in the area of Old Greenwich, Connecticut, close to the train station there. And, at times, Amtrak trains are often delayed because they have to travel behind Metro-North local trains. I wish that the commuter railroad would show some courtesy and stop that practice.

A Penn Station Primer – and New Jersey Transit

Back in 2017, a New Jersey Transit train derailed in Penn Station. The derailment was a little more than a minor one, but no one was killed. However, hundreds of people were forced to wait for some time before they were rescued. After that, there were several other derailments and a sideswipe incident of two trains, one Amtrak and one New Jersey Transit. None of these incidents were fatal but hundreds of thousands of people were caught up in the ensuing delays. The blame for these accidents were attributed to some worn out trackwork within the Penn Station terminal area. Amtrak was and is responsible for the maintenance of the tracks within the Penn Station area.

That much was said by Charles "Wick" Moorman, who was the president of Amtrak early in 2017. I remember the news conference in which Mr. Moorman, at the time, a recent dean of the freight railroad known as Norfolk Southern, blinked at the high powered New York media lights, and still told the truth.

But in the news media (I was watching WABC, channel 7, in New York) went right past that explanation and onto the frustration of the passengers.

Afterwards, Amtrak organized an expedited repair program on the Penn Station trackage. The program would require that both the Long Island railroad and New Jersey Transit suspend or reroute some of their trains from Penn to other terminals. Shortly after that, New York's governor Andrew Cuomo announced that the rebuilding plan and the rerouted commuter trains would add up to a "Summer of hell". A couple of media analysts wondered why Amtrak, with less than 10% of the passengers using Penn Station, was in charge of the place.

So, dear reader, please allow me to give to you this small, historic primer on why things are the way they are in Penn Station. There is little need to have a similar discussion on the nearby Grand Central station, as that property is occupied and run by only one railroad, Metro North.

Let us now rewind, way back into time, past the previous turn of the century, back into the turn of the century before that one (1899-1900). At that time, it was the railroads which were the primary form of overland transportation. New York City, then as now, was a place that everyone wanted to get to. Several different railroads approached New York from the West. These railroads had to terminal on the New Jersey side of the Hudson River at various points opposite Manhattan. Ferries were employed to take the passengers and freight that last mile to the city. Only the New York Central, which approached the city from the north, and the New Haven, which approached from the northeast, enjoyed the short lived monopoly of going directly to Manhattan.

Following the first successful train tunnel under the Hudson River, built for the Hudson and Manhattan (now today's PATH trains), the mighty Pennsylvania Railroad lined up financing for an even larger project. From the west, the railroad built two tunnels under the Hudson to mid- Manhattan (34th street), built the huge Penn Station edifice, and then continued east with four more railroad tunnels under the East river to Long Island. Later, the PRR, along with the New Haven railroad, built the Hell Gate Bridge from Queens to the Bronx. These huge undertakings were all done with private money. And the Pennsylvania Railroad once ran long distance passenger trains as well as commuter services to Long Island and New Jersey. Today, it takes three government entities to do the same job. Just sayin'.

In any case, the years went by and passenger trains went from a profitable business to a loss making business. Freight trains almost always made a profit but in many cases the freight trains were not profitable enough to cover the losses made by the passenger trains. Federal and State laws prevented the railroad from quickly exiting the passenger train business.

At the time, the answer was to merge and downsize the railroads. The PRR entered into a real estate deal that saw the destruction of the above ground Penn Station in 1963. Two years later the PRR sold the Long Island railroad to New York State. After that, the Pennsylvania railroad merged with the New York Central in 1968. The New Haven was added in 1969. Finally, the Federal Government (during the Nixon era!) saw the plight of the disappearing passenger train, and formed Amtrak in 1971 to take the nation's passenger trains off the backs of the freight railroads. Still, the new Penn Central railroad went bankrupt in 1972. A restructuring of the Penn Central properties was not to come until 1976 with the formation of the freight railroad known as Conrail.

In 1976, Amtrak was given nearly the entire Northeast Corridor, from Washington DC to Boston, MA, including Penn Station. A section from New Rochelle, NY to New Haven, CT remained under local (MTA) control. Still, at this time most commuter railroads basically oversaw the state financing of commuter trains run by the host railroad. Commuter railroads as we know them today did not come into being until 1983, when Congress directed that the states should take full responsibility for the commuter railroads from Conrail (which was receiving millions in Federal aid). As an aside, New Jersey Transit is celebrating its' 40th anniversary this year. This anniversary dates to 1979 when NJT took over most bus routes in New Jersey.

So, Amtrak was given control of Penn Station back when most self-operating commuter railroads didn't really exist. Only the Long Island railroad was running its' own trains while (for example, among others) Metro-North and the Boston MBTA were reimbursing the freight railroad Conrail for the costs of running the trains, until 1983. Today, Amtrak is the poor stepchild of passenger trains in the United States. The Federal Government keeps Amtrak on a starvation budget. Meanwhile, the commuter railroads get adequate (more or less) funding from their home states.

Amtrak

In this essay I will discuss Amtrak as it is in the present time. As of now (September, 2019) Amtrak is the poor stepchild of American passenger train railroading. New York State spends more on its' subways than the Federal Government spends on Amtrak each year. And, it has been this way for many years. However, this status quo cannot last much longer. Amtrak needs a significant amount of money in the near future just to update the passenger car fleet. Amtrak's signature passenger car in the East, the Amfleet coach, has been around since 1976. The double decked Superliner coach has been around since 1985. So far, this is not necessarily a bad thing, since both sets of passenger cars were old school American made. With a thorough rebuilding, both sets of cars can be made to last another 10-20 years. New locomotives are now on the horizon, and none too soon.

What is relatively new about Amtrak is the leadership that it now has. The new leadership and the top management were imported from the airline industry. Those who are currently in charge see the passenger railroad through the eyes of a former airline industry CEO.

From what I have read, the airline industry management has had two main effects upon Amtrak.

The main thing is that Amtrak will most likely break-even next year (2020) due to some relentless cost cutting. The current CEO has looked at every facet where Amtrak either makes money or spends money, and has either charged more or cut back. I have to agree that these actions were necessary. Amtrak should approach a break-even balance because this is how the entire country judges the railroad. Nearly every written article, especially those from financial publications, see Amtrak in this light. No one writes about how the Federal Government, and some states, subsidize other forms of transportation through infrastructure such as airports, highways and dredged waterways. No one even writes about how the Federal Government and some states directly subsidize airline service. But I will write about it, in the next essay.

So, Amtrak will break even in 2020. All of the above writers of those financial articles will hail the newest financial turnaround king. However, the former airline CEO and his airline cronies have not improved Amtrak. From what I have read, these airline industry managers take a dim view of the railroad advisory and enthusiast populations. They see these people as dummies who are stuck in the dim past.

But I see the airline heavy management as idiots of the present. Other than the numbers that put

Amtrak on a break-even par, which again is quite an achievement, there is the downgrading of the Amtrak service. They actually seem to think that Amtrak has something to learn from the airlines when it comes to handling passengers and dealing with people. Nothing can be further from the truth. Think about the crappy experience that flying is for most of us. While there is nothing that we can do about the TSA experience, what a person goes through at the airline gate is ridiculous. The waiting, and the pathetic airline boarding group apartheid, simply to crowd into the same aluminum tube, simply shows that flying SUCKS. Period.

When you are in a plane, in coach, you are entirely too close to the person around you. You are closer to that stranger, than you are to your spouse, and for a number of hours yet. No one really speaks to anyone on a plane. After the plane lands, people can't wait to leave the plane. Indeed, the passengers look as if they are evacuating the plane, instead of just leaving the plane. And this is the passenger experience that these ex- airline managers want to bring to the railroad??

This crap has already started, with Amtrak's efforts to restrict the dining car to the sleeping car passengers on the long distance trains, or replace the dining car entirely, with boxed meals. I realize that there is government legislation that restricts how much Amtrak can spend on dining car services. But this is the train, where you can spend days on board. Those at Amtrak should work on getting that legislation repealed.

The thing is, for me, if you as a person, cannot understand the train for what it is, you cannot improve the train to the potential that it has.

What I would do with Amtrak

So, what I would do if I had the responsibility of running Amtrak? There is a lot that I would do. The first thing that I would do is get any thought and idea that ever came from an airline about running a railroad out and away from Amtrak. This includes throwing out the silly emergency exit cards from the passenger car seatbacks. It includes removing former airline personnel. It would be necessary to inform everyone that Amtrak is about the passenger train, and nothing else.

The second thing that I would do is inform all of the present management, young and old, within the freight railroads that Amtrak is in fact, your stepdaughter. Amtrak was created to take over passenger service from the ailing railroads of the 1970's. I wonder if today's freight railroads, now fat with profits, could be convinced to reenter the passenger train arena! It could be said that Amtrak represents a kind of ongoing corporate welfare to the U.S. railroad industry. How would the freight railroads like it if they were forced to run passenger trains on their dime? I would especially take out the time to tell those who dispatch and run the trains on the freight railroad network a little more about Amtrak. The freight railroads should take some pride in running an Amtrak train on time just like they wish to run their freight trains on time.

The third thing that I would do is open up and employ a platoon of lobbyists who would see to it that Amtrak's interests are spoken for in Congress, and within the states that Amtrak trains run in.

I would bring up the little known fact that the Federal Government actually subsidizes air travel. They have been doing that for nearly as long as they have been subsidizing Amtrak. Since 1978, something known as the Essential Air Service has been paying for air service to small communities throughout the USA. Most of these communities are in Alaska. I have nothing against the Essential Air Service or the tiny communities that they serve. But no one seems to think about this as they excoriate Amtrak for its' subsidies. According to Wikipedia, Essential Air Service cost the government 283 million in 2016, the last year that they have tabulated.

I also would highlight the fact that the current appropriation for Amtrak falls far short compared to the amounts that New York State spends on the New York City subway and other countries expenditures upon their passenger railroads. The roughly 2 billion dollars that Amtrak receives each year, while nothing to sneeze at, compares poorly to what some

European countries spend. And the comparison becomes embarrassing when you consider the sizes of these European countries. A look at some dated information from Wikipedia online reveals some surprises. Germany, for example, spends about 17 billion Euros annually, about 18.8 billion dollars at the current exchange rate, on its' railroads. The size of Germany is about that of the state of Montana, although the population of about 83 million people speaks volumes about the amounts of public spending and the highly urbanized rail networks there. England spends about 4.4 billion Euros annually, converted from pounds, or about 4.8 billion dollars. England is about the size of Alabama. The population of that country is about 68 million. The American expenditure on passenger rail is the closest to Austria, which spent 2.3 billion Euros, about 2.5 billion dollars. Austria is roughly the size of Oregon. Austria has a population of about 8.8 million people. This is about equal to the population of New York City and Yonkers put together.

There are more than a few differences within these comparisons, especially when you consider population densities, environments, and the connections that each European country and the UK have to one another. Each of the countries that I have named also have what they call train operating companies that buy new rail equipment and pay a fee to run on tracks that are owned and maintained by the state. The train operating companies say that they are profitable because they do not pay the full costs to maintain or improve the railroad tracks, they just pay a fee, just like a trucker pays a highway toll. In the UK, all of the railroads there are train operating companies. But the UK taxpayer is still on the hook as far as maintaining the tracks as well as any expansion of the system. In Germany and Austria, the national railways dominate, but train operating companies exist there as well. In these two countries, the national railways claim to operate at a profit. Otherwise, the taxpayers in those countries will be on the hook.

Then again, we can look at some other extremes. New York state proposes to spend 10 billion dollars per year, for each of the next five years, on the MTA. In Japan, the railroad companies known as JR East, JR West and JR Central require no subsidy from the government. These passenger railroads (freight volume is less than 1% of all freight moved in Japan) are responsible for 60% of all passenger traffic in that country. Yes, they are that good.

The fourth thing that I would do is see if it were plausible to expand the Amtrak Auto train franchise. In this congested highway environment, there should be plenty of business available to Amtrak to make money, not just by hauling cars, but by hauling truck trailers full of freight as well. And since Amtrak owns most of the Northeast Corridor (Boston to Washington). I would start there. I only wish I knew what the costs are for the railroad to haul a passenger vehicle or a truck trailer. (I am talking about the Roadrailer, which was a truck trailer adapted for use within a train). And I wish I knew even more about that railroad.

The Media

Well.....yes, while we are at this, let us continue around the transit and railroad world with a look at the media. By this, I mean all of the media, and however we get our news.

Let's start with the newspapers. By this, I am talking about the New York Daily News, the Times, the Post, and the Long Island Newsday. By the way, we in the New York metropolitan area should consider ourselves lucky that we still have 4 major newspapers to choose from at this time.

All of these (and other) newspapers have reported on the subway system at various times and with varying degrees of intensity. Most of the time, the articles printed seemed like gap fillers in the space of the newspaper page. At times, some newspapers have had subway reporters who wrote articles only about the subways. All were regular guys who were assigned to the job. No one had the least bit of interest in any train or railroad. I could tell by their writings. Sometimes some news stories rise to the surface, such as the horrifying story of a man who leapt to his death in from of a number 4 train in the Bronx, carrying his 5 year old child with him. This happened in September 2019. Luckily, the child survived with only a scratch. I read the heart stopping newspaper accounts as well. But I could not find anything in any paper about how the train operator felt about this. But most of the time, news reports about most other things within the subways come across pretty mundane to the average reader, and are probably skipped over after a few sentences.

The one exception is the moutha-fucking New York Post. This paper has a long history of vilifying the transit worker at every possible turn. Especially heinous is the editorial section where every problem that the MTA has is somehow connected to its employees. Facts are hard to come by in the New York Post; when one does come across a factoid, it is often slanted out of proportion. The Long Island Railroad worker is often a special target of the paper, because they are often the highest paid employees in the MTA. The Post has taken what they think is excessive about LIRR compensation, and they intimated that all MTA employees get paid at this rate. It is interesting to note that in the Post's opinion, the LIRR pay rates have nothing to do with a very expensive Long Island. The transit and railroad unions get slammed as if they had the power that they had back in the 1970's still existed. I will never forget that the Post called us "RATS" when the transit union went on strike back in 2005.

And for weeks after the strike, the paper invited the passengers to take photos of sleeping station agent workers in their booths. No one, least of all that paper, tried to find out why this was going on. It was far better from that paper's point of view to depict all transit workers as lazy bums draining the state coffers. The reality was that the MTA was not replacing every station agent when someone called out sick. Then, the original station agent was stuck in that booth for another 8 hours, spouse and children be damned. Under these conditions, one would be hard pressed not to fall asleep! And I would how many people thought that something must be wrong – now they waited 14 years to find this out!

Within the New York Post is a little gray woman (I am not talking about the "gray lady" of the New York Times here) who has made it her life's work to denigrate MTA employees. Indeed, all public employees except the police and firemen have been targets of her ire. It seems to her that if only the MTA employees would get paid a minimum wage, all the MTA's problems would be solved. If only she would apply that reasoning to herself, and cut her salary in half, then the New York Post could sell for 50 cents.

And then, we can look at the Post's attitudes on race, and politics, and that infamous monkey cartoon spoofing former President Obama, etc., etc., and then wonder why anyone takes that newspaper seriously.

The Media, an Example.

I have said in the previous essay, when it comes to the subways in particular, and the railroads in general, that the media is often clueless, sometimes even when they have the facts. While this position reflects that of most of the public, it is up to the media, from whatever source that it came from, to place whatever facts that it has in context and to explain and enlighten the public with that news. This becomes even more important with a subject as dull (to the public) as subways and railroading. Note that I did not say that anything was "fake news" at least not here. But still, independent vetting and background checking is still critical, especially within the print medium.

I understand that the TV news reporter or the TV personality might not have time to check facts but they should offer an update if necessary.

It's a shame that most people don't even think about this, whether they shape and handle the news or when they consume the news. Within this book I have used newspaper articles from several sources. All of them contained the facts but many did not present these facts so that the reader gains anything from the story. In this book, I think that I have, and I think that the articles have more impact in the way I have presented them. This can be done while maintaining objectivity.

Now, I can take apart some crap like what appears almost daily within the Post. But let's look at something from the old Gray Lady, the New York Times. Background checking, and even simple observation, would have made a difference.

So it was when a New York Times reporter was brought into the West 4th Street Tower back in April, 2017. A story was printed in the New York Times on May 1, 2017, titled "6 Million Riders a Day, 1930's Technology". It was about the old signal equipment working within the West 4th Street tower; the age and reliability of that equipment was brought into question.

Before I get into that news story, let me tell you a little bit about that old West 4th Street tower. It was constructed back in the 1930's (yes, they got that right) back when this portion of the subway was known as the IND, or Independent subway lines. The city owned Independent lines was very expensive for its' time but what the city got back in return was a major portion of one of the top five railroads on Earth. That sentence is still the truth today.

West 4th Street tower was placed at a point where all of the former Independent lines that travel throughout the city (Except the G line in Brooklyn) come together. If necessary, any of the trains on the IND lines (today's A, C, and E trains upstairs and the B, D, and F trains downstairs) can be monitored, and if necessary, can be visited by a supervisor. Even after the merger of the IND lines with the BMT and IRT lines in 1940, the West 4th Street tower remained a critical junction within the Transit System. The tower was staffed by at least one supervisor and one tower operator around the clock.

Anyway, let's get back to that visit at the West 4th Street tower. I was not there, but I know what really happened. The Times reporter and a photographer were shepherded in there by an MTA "minder", like how some people have when you are visiting a foreign, repressive country. The "minder" could have come from one of the contractors. In any case, it was the "minder" who, by pointing out all that he or she thought was wrong with the current setup, influenced the reporter on what to write. The reporter, who had probably never even realized that anything like a subway control tower even existed until this time, dutifully wrote close to what she was "told", in so many handheld device applied words.

To the lay person, especially a younger person, the interior of the West 4th Street tower can be a confusing place. It is dark, there are desks and lockers and this one big iron object that dominates the space. The employees refer to it as the "Machine". On top of this machine are rows of lights, in several colors. These rows of lights can be deciphered by the tower operator as oncoming trains, among other things. The row of silver handles on the front of the machine control specific switches and signals within the tower's area of operation.

None of this was explained to the Times reporter. The supervisor and tower operator on duty at the time tried to make themselves small, and stay out of the photographer's range, and not engage the reporter. After all, they probably felt that the next day they would be depicted as lazy employees stealing the state money.

What happened was that in the Times' article, the tower was depicted as a backwards old museum from the 1930's. And in some people's minds, it could be taken that way. Except for one thing – that machine was doing its' job. Instead, a photo that was printed with the article has a caption that said "Much of the subway system's technology is so outdated that it cannot precisely identify where trains are". The thought that this sentence imparts is that this is one of the long neglected dungeons, deep within the transit system, that is the source of all of the problems and delays suffered by the transit riders. And, like some kind of Indiana Jones, working within the tombs, she apparently felt like she has discovered the source of the transit malaise. Let us now reality check this. An airplane traffic control center cannot identify, to the foot, precisely where the planes are. Neither does the GPS in your car or on your phone. It is usually off by 10 or 20 feet. That's not "precise", and no one is complaining about that, either. In the article, the CBTC, if it was installed, would eliminate the gap between trains (it won't, a minimum safety spacing between trains is necessary) thus allowing trains to run closer together. CBTC would, according to the article, be the savior of the New York City Transit world. It is true that the trains would run closer together using the CBTC system but the amount of new trains (2, maybe 3 more trains per hour) and direction is not worth the costs (in my opinion) of installing such as system. Nowhere in this article was the "precise" (let's use that term) costs of installing CBTC was mentioned. Thankfully the article did mention a little of what it takes to install the CBTC. The article does mention that the Transit Authority did ask for 3.2 billion dollars for "Signal and Communications Work", but that could be anything, not just CBTC.

Then, there is this. It's a little close to nit – picking, but it deserves to be mentioned. The article mentions that the CBTC system is also safer because trains "can be stopped automatically" and mentions the 1991 Union Square subway derailment in which five people were killed. The reporter apparently did not, and (I bet) still does not know about the mechanical stop arm of the legacy subway signal system. No doubt, the "minder" failed to mention this. The stop arm, that is raised when the subway signals are red, will stop a subway train. The 1991 subway accident mentioned in the article is a bad example. In that accident, the train operator derailed his train by going way too fast over a set of track switches. A red signal was never displayed in that accident. Furthermore, other subway systems that use computerized control, such as in Washington, DC, have had bad and fatal accidents while using their computer control.

I could go on and on, but hopefully, you get the point. More importantly, here is what the reporter failed to observe. The reporter failed to observe that the large, blinking machine was doing its' work, with the trains entering and leaving the station without a problem. The reporter failed to observe that all the ancillary objects with dust on them that aided the operation of the machine stayed dusty because they were reliable. The reporter failed to observe how that one tower operator could keep track of six subway lines on two levels, all with the 1930's signal technology. And apparently, the reporter failed to even ask any questions from the tower operator and the supervisor on duty, even if they were trying to avoid her. She could have gotten another perspective on the operation of the tower and the reliability of the legacy signal system.

In any case, since that news story appeared in the Times, the Post, which often bites the ass of the Times, also sent a reporter to the West 4th Street tower, about three weeks later. The result was probably much the same. Then, in a fit of total imbecility, the MTA choose to close the West 4th Street tower. The control of the trains in the West 4th street area has been transferred uptown, to 34th street and 6th avenue. Did anyone notice an improvement in how the trains are running there?

I don't think so. And the woman who wrote the article for the Times has received commendations and a prize for her work.

Only in New York.

In Conclusion

Well dear reader, thanks for having made it to the end of the book. I realize that the subjects of subways, trains and railroading, is deadly to most people, even if it has been a lifelong vocation and hobby to me. I hope that I have made this walk through the city's rail systems enlightening and maybe even a little entertaining at times.

I have made the New York City subways as my railroad subject of choice. This comes from my childhood, when most of the kids in the first car of the subway train choose to look out the front window. For me, there was no train on the planet better or faster than the No. 5 Thru Express. The No.5 train, after leaving the 180th Street station, went express through the Bronx, passing a number of local stops. The train seemed to sail as the Bronx apartment buildings went by. The next stop was underground at 149th Street and Third Avenue. That train was, in my mind, was the fastest and the best express train in the world. Today's imitation, hobbled by timing signals, is but a far cry from what that train was earlier.

I hope that the book will eventually reach enough people – enough people with power – so that we do not have to go down this insane road of spendthrift spending that will result in a boarded up and inaccessible subway for the next ten years. A subway that will not be materially different from the one that exists now. A subway that will show little for the billions and billions poured into it. A subway where the contractors will make hurried and stupid excuses to cover promises unfulfilled while they run out of town. Have you ever walked into a neighborhood subway station, and said to yourself, "Oh! They spent ten million dollars here!" No, I did not think so. Well there are actually a few examples, mostly in Manhattan. The three new stations of the Second Avenue Subway; and that hugely expensive sculpture of a station in lower Manhattan otherwise known as the Oculus. This station, known otherwise as the World Trade Center, somehow reminds me of a huge fish market, at least on the outside. And, I can think of one more - the Coney Island – Stillwell Avenue complex in Brooklyn. Here, at least, the ten million that you see (actually, that station costs much more) is being put to good use. The question will be for those of you who will end up detouring your commuting lives away is, can we afford the mess that they propose? Will we end up watching with envy the few that can resort to limos and helicopters? Meanwhile, the main result for most of us will be higher taxes and congestion fees – and absolute gridlock— for the rest of the city's working class.

I was born in this city, in the Bronx. Like most New Yorkers, I have a love/hate relationship with this city. I have grown up in this city, worked and now I have retired in this city.

I do not like that fact that New York City is no country for old men (or women). I do not like that fact that since I have retired, the more or less fixed income that I now have will be slowly overcome by inflation. I do not like that fact that I could trade in my little bitty house in the boroughs for a much larger and more comfortable home somewhere else. I wrestle with these facts every day, wondering whether to stay or to go.

Should I really be in another place, when I enjoy the fact that I where I live now, I can get a burger at 4am, on a whim? Where I can easily meet friends for a jaunt around the city? Where I could be exactly the person I want to be? Can I pause and watch a subway train, packed with living people full of life, pass by? Or will I have to relocate to the 'burbs and now be satisfied with looking at a rusty, dusty freight train full of scrap metal and graffiti? Or will I eventually be one of the many New Yorkers who return periodically from Podunk somewhere to get a whiff of the city?

We all ask ourselves these questions, and more, when it finally becomes "that time" to make a decision on leaving this city that we love.

But does this city love us back? Sometimes, I think that this city is turning into some kind of an old school Times Square whore, with the hands extended via forever rising real estate taxes and carefully hidden traffic cameras that don't really protect the schools (Who the hell is in "class" at 10pm?). The crazy rents have all but squeezed out the lower middle class. What was the middle class is now the lower middle class – whether they like it or not. And there is one more, unrelated thing that I have to say. The damn World Trade Center twin towers should have been rebuilt as twin towers, maybe in a different form, but rebuilt. To me, the current tower downtown will always be an acknowledgement that New York City is a little less than it once was. After all, which movie has used the new World Trade Center building as an establishing shot?

There is another reason why I wrote this book. This book is my comment on a part of New York that I know, the subway. This is my attempt on making the subway, which is an important part of the city, something a little less than insane.

In time, I can see myself "out there" somewhere, in a medium sized city, on a street with wide boulevards and intersections, listening to the radio in my car to a station playing old music. The traffic in these streets are calm. There is no problem rolling up slowly to a red light here – you don't have to try and beat the traffic signals. And then a song like "I am, I said" by Neil Diamond comes on. This ancient song is a ballad for all ex - New Yorkers. Listen to it sometime. I can see myself getting entranced by the lyrics of this song, at least until the car horns start blowing behind me.

Should this be the future of every retired New Yorker?

ABOUT THE AUTHOR

Torin Reid is a born and bred New Yorker who grew up in the Bronx. He is a six year Army veteran, having served in Germany, and he has worked 28 years for the New York City subway. During this time Mr. Reid wrote magazine articles about urban rail and bus transportation for that past 30 years for various rail transportation journals. Motorman's Rant is Mr. Reid's second book, following his 2016 book Advice for Men about the American Woman.

Torin Reid presently lives in Queens in New York City along with his two sons, Torin Jr., and Robert Andrews. He spends his with his sons as well as banging some nails on the house every now and then, and doing some writing.

If you would like to leave a comment about this book, please use the following email address: Bradley17Moore@gmail.com. Bradley Moore is the author's pen name. Comments may be used in a subsequent publication. There is presently no other authorized email address for Torin Reid

Printed in the United States
By Bookmasters